THE TRUMPET VOICE OF INDIA

THE TRUMPET VOICE OF INDIA

SPEECHES OF

Babu Surendranath Banerjea

DELIVERED IN ENGLAND, 1909

BY

SURENDRANATH BANERJEA

GYAN

Published by

GYAN

Gyan Publishing House
5, Ansari Road
Daryaganj, New Delhi-110002
Phone: 011-47034999, 9811692060
E-mail: books@gyanbooks.com

Distribution Network
gyanbooks.com
India, USA, Canada, UK, Australia, France

ISBN: 978-81-212-8198-0 (PB)
First Published, 1909

2nd Impression 2023

Printed at: Gyan Press, Delhi.

THE TRUMPET VOICE OF INDIA
Author: SURENDRANATH BANERJEA

BABU SURENDRANATH BANERJEA

THE TRUMPET VOICE OF INDIA

SPEECHES OF

Babu Surendranath Banerjea

DELIVERED IN ENGLAND, 1909

MADRAS

GANESH & CO., PUBLISHERS

CONTENTS

PUBLISHERS' NOTE

In this volume are brought together the speeches made by Babu Surendranath Banerjea during his recent visit to Britain as the Indian delegate to the Imperial Press Conference. These speeches form a landmark not only in the life (by no means uneventful) of the distinguished patriot but also in the fortunes political of his mother country. Speaking from the vantage ground of an invited guest of the British people, he spoke with an authority and was listened to with a deference which he could otherwise not have commanded in spite of all his undoubted oratorical powers. That the popular leader made an effective use of this unique opportunity, is proved, among other ways, by the vigorous campaign started and carried on by some retired Anglo-Indian officials of high and low repute, living on pensions paid out of the Indian taxpayers' money, to discredit the messenger in order thereby to discount his message. This was only to be expected. There could not be much love lost between administrators whose lack of sympathy with Indian aspirations is the root cause of the present unrest in India and the gifted patriot who has done so much to foster those aspirations. But what can these venomous critics do ? The herald has proclaimed the wants and wishes of his people—of Indians generally and of the Bengali race in particular—in trumpet tones whose resonance is slow and hard of dying in the ears of Englishman and Indian alike.

This is our apology, if apology is needed, for publishing these epoch-making speeches in a convenient and portable size.

Babu Surendranath's first two speeches made in the Imperial Conference were evoked, one in a spirit of reverential appreciation and the other in the style of a spirited defence, by the discourses of two eminent statesmen, one of whom has given unmistakable proofs of his sympathy with popular aspirations in India as elsewhere, and the other is a dignified replica of Lord Curzon. Lord Morley's speech on Literature and Journalism is worth reading for its own sake as well as for the background it furnishes to Babu Surendranath's first speech in England; and for the full understanding of the second it is necessary to read Lord Cromer's attack on the Press in India and Egypt. Hence the inclusion in this volume of both Lord Morley's and Lord Cromer's speeches at the Imperial Press Conference.

LORD MORLEY

THE

IMPERIAL PRESS CONFERENCE

LORD MORLEY

LITERATURE AND JOURNALISM

Gentlemen,—I thank you for the heartiness of your reception—a heartiness partly due, I dare say, to the fact that I have myself been for a good long spell of time a member of the profession which many of you represent. (Hear, hear.) I observe in the "Times" to-day that you are a little jealous of the restrictions of time to such a subject as Literature instead of giving a still further time to those great problems of Imperial defence which have hitherto taken up all your attention. Well, I quite see the oddity, so to call it, of appending a discussion upon Literature to the great topics that you have hitherto been dealing with. But Literature, after all, is not a very small topic. (Hear, hear.) There is a connection, if you will let me say so, between Literature and Empire. (Cheers.) I only offer a commonplace upon that point, as if our glorious English tongue were not one of the glories of Empire—(hear, hear)—as if it were not perhaps the strongest, the most enduring bond of Imperial Union—aye, and possibly a thousand times stronger and more enduring and wider in a sense, wider and deeper Imperially than all the achievements, magnificent as they are, of all the soldiers and sailors and of the statesmen who have directed them. (Hear, hear.) To go on with my commonplace—as if Shakespeare, and Burns and Bunyan, and Swift, and all the rest of that superb gallery were not the greatest of British Empire builders. (Cheers.) This is only a commonplace but a commonplace with a true and deeper grandeur in it and I know not in the history of mankind of a more stupendous—I had almost said more overwhelming—act than the supreme domination of the English tongue over millions in the new worlds of the West and in the ancient worlds of the East. (Hear, hear.) It is a stupendous and overwhelming fact, and that, I think, justifies the place which you have been good enough to give Literature among the objects of your consideration. (Cheers.) I will make one remark on the other side. I am rather surprised that you did not choose—or those who had the choice of the topics did not choose—science as one of your subjects, because, after all, the governing thoughts and the moving interests of men fluctuate with the ebb and flow of the great tides of human curiosity and energy, and passion and interest. One age is more specially an ecclesiastical or a theological age; another is a political age; a third is a literary age; but I do believe you will all agree with me that the age in which we live, in which we find ourselves, is before all else, alike in its practical and in its speculative bearings, a scientific age. Therefore, if you had had to-day a discussion upon the science of the Empire I am not at all sure—it need not have been introduced by me—but I am not at all sure that you could not have got a more apt and directly profitable discussion. Now I am not going to regale you with all the things—the grand and noble things—that have been said about Literature. I am not certain that my best plan would not have been to wander about my library for an hour or two and make a collection of the things that have been said about Literature. But that is not our object to-day.

We are to-day to talk of the connection between literature and journalism. What is a journalist ? It is not easy to say ; It is not quite easy to say off-hand what literature is—a power, a force, a symbol, an interpretation ? Are you going to treat it in your discussion to-day as a profession ? I think you probably will be inclined to regard that as the view that is most appropriate for this occasion. Well, I looked out, as my wont is, when I am perplexed over a definition—I looked out the word 'literature' in that splendid monument of learning and effort—the "Oxford Dictionary"—and I hope everyone of you possesses it on his shelves, for in that monument you will find many things which make extremely good reading. I turned to "Literature," and what was my shock to find myself quoted, and thereby, at any rate, handed down to immortality—(laughter)—as having said that "Literature is the most seductive, the most deceiving, and the most dangerous of all professions " (Loud laughter).

It is a long time since I committed myself to that perplexing opinion. But we survive our own power of thought, no doubt and I have survived that end. I cannot recover the secret of that menacing language (Laughter) I was thinking of the other day. I believe it was a feeling I had in my mind at that date an enormous number of persons—I use the word " persons " to include women as well as men—that an enormous number of persons were committing themselves to literature as a profession who had no more right to take to the writing of books than Mr. Birrell and I have to take to painting oil pictures or water-colours (Laughter). So many think themselves called, so few find themselves, or are found by the public, really chosen (Laughter). As to the profession—the honourable, the arduous profession of a journalist—you know Carlyle used very different language from that. "Is not every able editor," he said, "a ruler of the world, being as he is a persuader of it." But then he said, on another occasion when some young friend told him he was going to embark upon journalism: "Oh," he said, "journalism is ditch-water" (Laughter). Sometimes I am inclined to think that it is (Renewed laughter). But the class of men of letters more strictly so called contains an infinite variety of general and species and sub-species from the high class publicist, who is the real persuader of the people and the real ruler of the world down to my humble friends who purvey leaderettes and nimble paragraphs. What are we here to-day to confer about? We are not to confer. I take it, upon grammar, though it is a fruitful topic; nor punctuation, as to which I have not a single word or thing to say to anybody—(Laughter)—not as to whether you are to use the relative pronoun "which" or "that," we are not here to discuss style. Nobody can make a motion, or move an amendment, I fancy upon "style" (Laughter). Therefore we are not here for that. I will only make one remark about style and I hope you will all agree with me, we cannot—you and I—we cannot approach in stature and compass all the giants; but there is one thing we can do. We can strive in our pursuit, in our cultivation of the great, the noble, the difficult art of writing—we can strive after, at all events, the two moderate virtues of simplicity and directness. And by simplicity and directness, I mean of course freedom from affectation, because affectation is the most odious of qualities in character and manners, and I think it is even more odious still in literature and journalism. Therefore I hope you aim, as I think you do, at the simple and direct, as everyone of us ought to aim and everyone of us can, if we take the proper trouble to attain it. Of course, the foundation of style is a full knowledge of matter. It was said of platform speakers that platform speeches depended on three things:—First, "Who says it;" second "How he says it"; and third "What he says"; and really it was added that what he said was the least important of the three (Laughter). That is not true of the journalist, because what a platform speaker says vanishes more or less rapidly, but what the journalist writes remains, and therefore it is that what he says is as important as the fact that the individual writer says it and the way in which the individual writer says what he has got to say. Now journalism, I was told the other day by an eminent member of the Conference—a home member—that journalism is literature in hurry and he taxes me with having invented that saying. I don't agree with it (Laughter). You have got to go a great deal deeper than that. I should say that the quality of literature, if it has one particular quality more than another in this regard, is that it is not in a hurry. Journalism is and must be in a hurry. Literature is not Literature that deals with the permanent element of human things. The journalist has to take the moods and occasion of the hour and make the best he can of them. Literature more or less prescribes the attitude of the judge. The journalist dealing more or less with what we call two issues is more or less an advocate. Literature deals with ideals ; the journalist is a man of action. Though he is a man of the pen, he is also a man of action—he is not a student, a scholar but a man of action—and therefore he is concerned with the real, though if he is a wise journalist as we all are (Laughter) he will understand that what he takes for the real or must take for the real is not half so real as a great deal of what is ideal. (Hear, hear and cheers.) Would anybody deny that there are about half a dozen lines of Burns which have been more quoted upon political thought and action than all the millions of leading articles that have been written in Burns's country and even in the southern part of the island? (Hear, hear.) But far more it is the business of literature to furnish a care for conventional rhetoric. The journalist must more or less follow conventional rhetoric ; but when all is said—I am not going to detain you—when all is said, the literary element in its best and widest sense is what makes all the difference in the world between the editor or the writer and the newsboy who is shouting scare headlines at the street corner. (Laughter). It is the presence in the mind, among the talents of the editor and his writers, the presence of literary elements in them, obviously, which makes the difference between them and the juvenile newsmonger.

I was challenged the other day to define what I understood by a good journalist and my friendly challenger tried his own hand at the qualities of a good journalist, and they appear to be candour, courtesy, independence, responsibility. Well, but these are qualities which go to the making not only of a good journalist, but to any decently good sort of man. (Laughter.) Therefore I find that definition quite inadequate. I am not going to attempt to specify the qualities of a good journalist, because I am rather afraid of you, and if I leave any qualities out, or put in any qualities which any individual among you possesses, or does not possess, I may make him an enemy for life—(Laughter)—and I am much too experienced to desire to make an enemy of anybody or any newspaper. (Laughter.) I have got a suggestion. Cromwell, in an interview that he had with a certain band of Presbyterian ministers said to them: "My brethren, I beseech you in the name of Christ, is it possible that you may be mistaken?" And I wonder whether in some journals I am acquainted with whether it would not be a good thing to have that saying of Cromwell's written in letters of gold in the editorial rooms—not the news room, but the editorial rooms—in all editorial rooms of newspapers.

A very eminent member well known to some of us here and to myself has for his telegraphic address, I observe, the word " Vatican." (Laughter.) Important as this Council is, I hope nobody will suppose that we are here to-day—that we are assembled at anything like a Vatican Council, going to proceed to define infallibility. Infallibility is generally impenitence—(Laughter)—and I hope nobody here is so unwise as to make any claim to it. But it is a comfort, as journalism is not infallible, that it is not omnipotent. It is not quite so omnipotent as it often thinks. When it talks of its power I am the last man to deny or to depreciate, but—I will not go into party politics—I cannot but recollect the two greatest elections—whether wise or foolish elections—in my time. They were the elections of 1880 and the nearer election of 1906 and I make bold to say that neither in 1880 nor in 1906 did the great leading organs of opinion—either metropolitan or provincial—did they anticipate or had they prepared for the verdict which the country, wisely or unwisely, arrived at. (Hear, hear.) I could say a bit more on that point but it would bring me into dubious ground. Now I want to say this, not the least because I want to say anything flattering—because I have no authority to flatter—but in my day the improvement in all respects in British Journalism—with Overseas Journalism I am less conversant—the improvement in all the vital aspects of what journalism ought to be has been enormous—(hear, hear)—and it has been enormous in a way which leads me confidently to expect that that improvement will still further extend. The old journalism—even in the high-class reviews for which you used to pay five or six shillings—was very coarse—I mean to say very rough and unsparing—and it was very ignorant, extremely ignorant. (Hear, hear.) When a writer addresses Wordsworth when he produced a poem and says, "Really, Mr. Wordsworth, this will never do"—(Laughter)—while another criticises the "Endymion" in the same sort of spirit—what can be more intolerable to think of? Well that is gone. It is true there is plenty of stiff language used. I remember once I was in charge of a newspaper there came to me a youngster who sought work or employment.

I said, "Any special quality?" Yes, he thought he had, "Well, what is it?" I asked. He said: "Invective." (Loud laughter.) "Well," I said, "invective is an admirable gift. Any particular form?" "No," he replied, "general invective." (Renewed laughter.) I think I observe one or two quarters where I believe my friend must have found employment since. (Loud laughter and applause.) I think everybody who observes as I have done—naturally it having been my profession—I think everybody will agree that the temper of journalism has enormously improved. It is not always—in politics, at all events—the climate is not always genial, but it is not ungenerous. Take it as a whole, the climate is not ungenerous. As for literary criticism—which is a matter we are more concerned with here to-day—there has never been, in my opinion either in this country or in France—where they have cultivated criticism to an extent that we have never applied ourselves to—there has never been much critical power and knowledge as you will find in half a dozen quarters in English journalism to-day. (Applause.) I must take care, for

I read—as I came up to-day—I read a review in a quarter which we all of us look to with respect in the field of literature, and observed a little remonstrance and a little complaint, writing about Shakespeare and other masters, that he is too modest and too cautious, and this modesty and caution move us, the writer says, to a little impatience of his hesitations and his delays.

I am sure—and I must be careful—that there is not a better critic than the gentleman who wrote that. I am sure there is not. There is no impatience in the best kinds of English criticism to-day with moderate and considered judgments (Hear, hear). Now I want to ask one or two questions of you. Your knowledge of the Press covers a wider area than mine. Is the Press, is the newspaper, the enemy of the book ? Do people in Australia, in England—wherever you like—read more books? Do they know better difference between a bad book and a good one ? I have known more than one man of great eminence who did not seem to think it much mattered—that a book was a book. (Laughter.) A friend of mine achieved great eminence in spite of that curious and extraordinary view. In my opinion, the answer to this question about the book—whether people read more and know better the difference between a bad book and a good book—the answer is, to the best of my knowledge and belief, thoroughly favourable and encouraging. There may be some gentleman here who has written a book which has not been a success. (Laughter.) There may be. Well, the book is its own enemy. It may come too soon or too late; the author may have minted a coin which is not in currency, or, like fruit and flowers in a garden he may have planted his thoughts—he may have chosen his season wrong, but the general result in my view is that in the matter of literature, the authors of books were never more favourably placed. (Applause.) One more question which is more important, perhaps. This place is, I am sure, the British Foreign Office and a conference of journalists; this is the Palace of Truth; and, therefore, I more confidently expect your views to be freely given upon this. It is said of critics of democracy, not merely in this country but elsewhere in other democracies, that journalism of the newer type impairs and weakens the faculty and habit of coherent and continuous attention. If it were so it would be a disaster. But anybody who thought about it, is aware that the faculty of continuous attention is one of the main gains of all education, I am not sure I would not say, it is not as much a gain from education as the knowledge itself which education implies. Is it true that the newer type of journalism weakens the faculty of coherent attention? I am bound to say that when I see gentlemen coming up to town of a morning in the suburban trains with a financial paper under the one arm and a sporting paper under the other, and a general paper, written what is called crisply—(Laughter)—and then, if he is of an æsthetic turn of mind, he has also an illustrated paper; and when I am told that this gentleman is having his character shaped and his opinions moulded and his views settled by this process, I confess I am very sceptical (Laughter). Well, you may think differently, and may not have observed that, after all, it is a question of practical observation whether the discursive character of some new types of journalism—whether that discursive character is, or is not fatal to effective and continuous attention. do not think I have any more to say, gentlmen; I have kept you too long as it is. ("No, no."). I will conclude with one remark. During your proceedings, a good deal has been said of the re-barbarisation of Europe—the rattling back into arms and to preparation for the use of arms. Herbert Spencer for a long time had noticed this tendency to re-barbarisation. I wonder how far the Press has a share in the large flow of general forces that have brought and are bringing this about. There are those who say that, though a Minister may make a blunder, though a permanent official may wear his official blinkers too large and too tight, though diplomatists may be not crafty enough or too crafty, that though personal egotism may blind our statesmen to larger considerations, yet the Press is more answerable than all these things put together. I have heard that view expressed and as I am putting one or two questions to you I will put that question to you: whether you consider that the influence of the Press overseas and at home—the influence of the Press—is systematically and perseveringly used on behalf of peace—of peace among the nations? Well, you will see. I will only say this—that nobody can avoid—here is nobody who is not bound to recognise that the Press is a great centre and fountain of public-hearted duty and moral force; that it is the guide to an intellectual grasp of the facts of the world; and thirdly that it is in its best forms an organ of practical commonsense. Gentlemen, I am very proud to have met you and I am always very proud to have been a member of your profession. (Loud cheers.)

BABU SURENDRANATH BANERJEA

Mr. SURENDRANATH BANERJEA in the course of the discussion said :—My Lord and Gentlemen,—In the observations which your lordship was pleased to address to us, and which all listened to with great interest and attention, and if I may add for myself without impertinence, with very great admiration, you referred to the predominance of the English tongue. My lord, nowhere is that predominance more marked than in my own country. The English language has been the means of uniting the varied races and religions, the peoples and complexities of our multiform civilisation in the golden chains of indissoluble union. It is our *Lingua Franca* and common means of communication, north, south, east, and west. All are bound together by the common medium of the English language. Under the influence of the English language and English literature—and in this matter I am not guilty of the slightest exaggeration when I say that in India the dry bones of the valley have become instinct with life—English language and literature have brought about the most stupendous transformation in the lifetime of our generation. New ideas have taken possession of men's minds. New impulses have filled their hearts, and a new spirit is visible in the land. English language and English literature has communicated the Promethean spark which has galvanised us into a new life. This is one of the most glorious achievements of the English race in the East. We had no newspapers before the establishment of British control. The first newspaper which was in India was published in 1817 and in Bengal. Thus in this, as in other matters, I am proud to say that my province has taken a lead. The Press has controlled the judgment, the conscience, the mind, and the religion of all India. Being of British origin it partakes of the virtues and of the defects of its parentage. Its heredity is marked on every phase of the situation. There is no quality for which the Britisher—and when I speak of the Britisher I include his kinsman over the seas—there is no quality for which the Britisher is more noted than the variety of his grumbling. He is a past master in the art, and therefore it is no wonder that that great authority, Sir William Hunter, has described the Native Press as "His Majesty's Opposition, always in Opposition." I dissent from that view completely. On the contrary, we are often proud to support the Government and accord to it a whole-hearted measure of support. And, my lord, if I may refer to a personal event I hope and trust that I may be excused. The whole of the Indian Press welcomed with enthusiasm and gratitude your lordship's scheme of reform on behalf of India. For we felt it to be a distinctly genuine effort on the part of the Government to associate the democracy with the administration of India. We did not, indeed, get all that we want. For instance, we wanted the power of the purse, but we did not get it. At the same time, we believe that it was a notable advance in the process of evolution which is bound to give us a definite, effective, and real measure of self-government. We are not under any illusions. We knew perfectly well the limitations of the scheme. But the Government provided the machinery which would enable the Government to place itself in touch with popular opinion and would enable the representatives of the people to exercise an effective measure of indirect pressure on the Government and, therefore, we felt that it was a scheme which ought to be welcomed. We felt that if we were patient and persevering, we should, in time, get what we wanted and be admitted into the great confederacy of free states acknowledging England as their august mother. Here at any rate there was no opposition, but absolutely whole-hearted support. My lord, the Indian Press is the youngest branch of the Imperial Press and I claim for it that it is the promising scion of a noble stock. God grant that it may increase in power, in strength, and in usefulness and responsibility, to the great credit of ourselves and the glory of the great Empire to which we all have the honour to belong.

LORD CROMER'S ATTACK ON THE INDIAN PRESS

Mr. McKenna and Gentlemen,—This important meeting of Colonial journalists certainly constitutes one of many proofs which have been afforded of late years of the great desire of all English-speaking subjects to be bound together in the closest bonds of union. Certainly there can be no class of persons more capable of being efficient agents to summon to communion than those who represent that great principle—the principle of free discussion which it has been our privilege to disseminate throughout the civilised world. But, gentlemen, I think it has to be remembered that, besides some twelve or thirteen millions of our own countrymen who live overseas, there are some 350 millions of subjects of the Crown who are not bound to us by any ties of race, religion, or common origin. They are bound to us to a certain extent by the ties of a common language—which on one side is an acquired language—for many of the Asiatics and Eastern subjects of the Crown have shown their special aptitude in the study of English; though I perhaps may be permitted to say, without offence, that in some few cases they have perhaps not made the best possible use of their linguistic knowledge when it has been acquired. Gentlemen, one of the greatest Imperial problems of the future is how these huge communities are to be governed. It is amongst these that I have spent some thirty-five years of my life –(cheers)–and let me say that during these thirty-five years I do not think any subject has caused me greater doubt and anxiety than the extent to which our cherished principle of freedom of discussion should be applied in cases of this sort. I approached the subject originally from the point of view of an English Liberal, and let me say of deep interest in the welfare of all those Eastern populations which in any way are brought in contact with Great Britain—if that constitutes a claim to be an Oriental Liberal, I lay claim to that title. (Cheers.) Approaching, therefore, the subject from the point of view of an English

Liberal, I always felt an instinctive dislike to restrictive or repressive measures. More than this, I was very fully convinced of the unwisdom of doing anything to encourage the taste which is rather common nowadays—the taste of political martyrdom that is a good deal stimulated by the fact that the sufferings of the political martyrs are not very acute. (Laughter.) I was glad to fall back on generalities such as " The liberty that degenerates into license can do no harm." "The truth will prevail," "Safety valves are necessary," and so on. (Laughter.) Actuated by these very laudable principles during many years, I did whatever little was in my power to prevent the editors of vernacular papers to a slight extent in India and to a greater extent in Egypt, from running the risk of committing journalistic suicide. (Laughter.) I cannot say, upon the whole, that my endeavours, and the endeavours of many others who agreed with me were very successful. Gentlemen, last year I had to get up in the House of Lords and make a speech which I will ask you to believe me caused many a bitter pang. I had to own that my views had been too optimistic and that the Press in these countries of which I am now speaking, although it does unquestionably a certain amount of good, does a great deal of harm and further that in these countries on the whole a greater amount of supervision was necessary than any to which we are accustomed. In point of fact in the countries of which I speak, which were some of them but yesterday governed under a system of extreme despotism, the great experiment of free discussion has to be tried under conditions which it is difficult to realise by those who agree with the air of freedom. Let me give you an illustration of what I mean by referring to the career of a very distinguished man, with whose name you will all be familiar, and who was both a journalist and a statesman—I mean Mr. David Sime. I do not profess to agree with all Mr. David Sime's views. Mr. Sime has been called the father of Australian Protection. Now, I am the son, or perhaps it is more correct to say the grandson of Free Trade—(cheers)—and after reading a very remarkable record of Mr. Sime's strenuous life I may say I am not more inclined than ever I was before to disown my parentage

(Laughter). However that may be, nobody could withhold admiration for his interesting and manly courage. He was a stout type, and he gave hard knocks to those with whom he disagreed, but he was also very fair, and nobody could read his works without being convinced of the fact that his opinions, whether right or wrong, were the result of honest and sincere conviction. What I want to say is that the East, so far as I know it, is not prolific in David Sime's. The soil is not congenial to their growth : and that I think is a prominent fact which was to be taken into consideration in the application and the test of theories, whether connected with social or political objects.

Gentlemen,—I feel, in presenting these remarks to you, that I labour under one serious disadvantage, for I appear before you to a certain extent as an *advocatus diabolus*. That is to say, in addressing an audience which more especially represents the principles of freedom of discussion, I think it my duty to say to you, as the result of my experience, that in certain parts of the British Empire the circumstances have to be taken into account in the application of that principle.

I trust you will pardon my frankness. (Cheers.) I am very glad to see there are some Indian delegates here, and I trust that before this Conference closes—for I am sorry I have to go away myself—they will give us the benefit of their opinion on this special subject. I hope more specially that they will tell us whether there is any real connection between some of the unquestionably wild writing in a section of the vernacular Press of India and the commission of those dastardly outrages which have recently shocked all classes in this country, and have, I am sure, shocked the best of the British and native community in India. (Hear, hear, and cheers.) I cannot help for my own part fearing that some such connection could be established, but I would like before I sit down to add that I should be extremely glad if I am convinced that I am wrong (Hear, hear).

MR. BANERJEA'S SPIRITED DEFENCE

I am sorry to interpose with some observations which may not appear to be very pertinent to the question we are just considering; but an invitation was extended to us—I will not use the word challenge—by Lord Cromer that we should say whether in our opinion the anarchical developments which have recently taken place in Bengal are due to the irresponsible utterances of a certain section of the Indian Press. Sir, to that query, to that question, my answer is an unqualified and an emphatic "No." I will not defend what has been said in the Press. I say to my brother journalists gathered from all parts of the Empire—let me put this question to them. Are they prepared to defend everything in the Press—that is written in the Press—on questions of public importance? Are we an infallible body? Do we not commit great and gorgeous mistakes which we have reason to deplore to the end of our lives? I am not here to defend the irresponsible utterances which unfortunately have found a place in some of the Indian newspapers. But, Sir, let me say this, that some of these newspapers form a very insignificant minority; their circulation is limited; their hold upon the people is circumscribed. Let me not for one moment be understood as standing up here in justification of these anarchical developments. I express the sense of my province, of the better mind of Bengal and of India, when I say that we deplore these anarchical developments; we have condemned them in our columns with all the emphasis we can command. They are in entire conflict with those deep-seated religious convictions which consciously or unconsciously govern our every-day lives. And without offence may I be permitted to say that anarchy is not of the East, but of the West? It is a noxious growth which has been transplanted from the West to the East, and I hope and trust that under the salutary and ameliorating treatment of Lord Morley these anarchical developments will be utterly crushed out. (Cheers.) Sir, I am precluded from entering into controversial matters, or else I should like to say a word or two with reference to those circumstances which have led to these anarchical developments. But I recognise the fact that this is a non-controversial Conference, and I resist the temptation I exercise, the self-control of the East in this matter. (Laughter and cheers.) In conclusion, I desire to say this, that we regard the liberty of the Press as one of the greatest boons that have been conferred upon us under British rule. It was conferred on us not merely for political purposes but as an instrument for the dissemination of knowledge and of useful information. That was at any rate the conception of the great liberator of the Press, Lord Metcalfe, whose memory we cherish in our grateful recollections. Replying to a deputation which waited on him after the liberation of the Press, Lord Metcalfe said: "We are here not merely to collect taxes and to make good the deficit; we are here for a higher and nobler purpose, and that is, to pour into the East the knowledge, the culture, and the civilization of the West" (Cheers). That was the great aim, the great hope, the great aspiration of the liberator of the Press and that hope, that aspiration has been largely fulfilled. It is one of our greatest aims—I will claim this on behalf of my countrymen—that on the whole we have used it to the benefit of the Government, to the credit of our race; and long may it be enjoyed to the mutual advantage of England and India, and to the glory of both countries (Cheers).

SPEECH AT MANCHESTER

The delegates to the Imperial Press Conference visited Manchester where they were entertained at luncheon by the Lord Mayor and Lady Mayoress.

The toast of the luncheon, as proposed by the Lord Mayor, was the Imperial Press, coupled with the name of Mr. Surendranath Banerjea.

Mr. Banerjea, who was received with loud cheers, said :—

My Lord Mayor, Ladies, and Gentlemen,—On behalf of my brother-delegates, as well as on my own behalf, I desire to thank you very heartily for the kind terms in which the toast has been proposed and the cordiality with which it has been accepted. From the moment we set foot here as the guests of the Committee of the Imperial Press Conference, and in a wider sense of the British public, we have been overwhelmed with an effusion of kindness and hospitality which, so far as I am concerned, has produced an indelible impression on my mind. The cordiality of our reception, and that by all parties, irrespective of political differences and the splendour of the hospitality which has been extended to us will be among our most grateful recollections. (Hear, hear.) And speaking as an Oriental, possessed of the warm susceptibilities of our race, I will say this, that so far as I am concerned, these pleasing memories will endure so long as life endures. To me, as an Indian delegate, a special measure of consideration has been shown, for which I am deeply grateful. May this feeling of personal kindness deepen into a widespread and enduring sentiment of sympathy for the great and ancient race to which I am so proud to belong, and whose destinies you now control. Speaking at Manchester, I permit myself to entertain this hope with some measure of confidence, for I remember that Manchester has always been the home of progressive ideas, that it is associated with the honoured names of Cobden and Bright and that it is the cradle of that school of politicians whose principles may now be challenged but whose achievements in the past cannot be questioned. For the last few days at the sittings of our Conference we have been talking of the Empire and of Imperial considerations. No theme could be more appropriate for an Imperial Press Conference ; and here let me press for the preferential treatment of the claims of my country ; not indeed commercially, for Manchester would scout the idea, but in a political sense. For India, in the words of a late Viceroy, is the pivot of the Empire and she is undoubtedly the brightest jewel in the Crown of England. (Applause.) May she long continue to be so, through the justice of British laws, the righteousness of British administration, the operation of that kindly and practical sympathy which more than laws and edicts bring the people nearer to their rules and bind them both in the golden chains of an indissoluble union. (Applause.) Great anticipations have been formed of our Imperial Conference by responsible persons, great results are expected to flow from its sittings. Whether these anticipations will be realised or not is it impossible to say, for the future is in the lap of the gods and I will not embark upon the venturesome task of unravelling its mysteries. But this I will say—and here I stand upon firmer ground free from the perils and embarrassments of prophesies and even of intelligent anticipations—that never was the sense of Imperial unity more forcibly demonstrated. (Applause.) It is a unity which extending from the heart of the Empire embraces the most distant units of the Imperial system and includes not only the self-governing States which have sprung from the loins of the parent-country, but the remote dependencies which have not yet attained to that political status. In the orderings of Providence, for good or for evil—for good, as I verily believe—the destinies of 300 millions of my countrymen, not savages or barbarians, but the representatives of a great and ancient civilisation—(applause)—have been entrusted to the care and keeping of the people of these islands. Never was a nobler trust or a more sacred function assigned to a great and Imperial race. God grant that this solemn trust, this awful responsibility, may be so discharged as to conduce to the permanent benefit of India and the lasting glory of England.

We have heard in these festive gatherings the strongest notes of loyalty struck by the delegates who have come from beyond South Africa, the representatives sometimes of a culture and civilisation different from those of the Mother-Country, have expressed their fervent devotion to the Empire and their unflinching determination to stand by the flag in the hour of emergency and danger. The history of these islands has been a history of great and unexampled prosperity and happiness; may it long continue to be so. For England has been the guide, the leaders the instructress of mankind in the difficult art of self-government. But should even a crisis arise—I will not say disaster—I desire to say, on behalf of my countrymen—and I am entitled, to speak with authority in their name—that we in India will not be wanting in our duty by the Empire (Applause). An ounce of fact, they say, is worth a ton of theory; and let me here refer to an incident—not drawn from the domain of the imagination, or the debatable land which separates truth from fiction—which will strongly confirm the view I am endeavouring to put forward. There occurred in 1885 what is known as the Pendjeh incident. Pendjeh is a small town on the Afghan frontiers. There in 1885 a brush took place between an Afghan outpost and some Russian soldiers. The incident, trivial as it was, threatened to involve England and Russia into war. For some time the rumours of war were persistent. At this juncture, I will not call it a crisis, the Indian Press—that section of it which I have the honour to represent at this Conference—appealed to our countrymen to offer themselves as volunteers for the defence of their hearths and their homes. In response to this appeal 500 young men of Calcutta, all of them in positions of respectability, some of them in the positions of light and leading, applied to the Government to be enlisted as volunteers. I myself was an applicant; and about that time, addressing a public meeting of my countrymen, I used language which I with your permission reproduce now as illustrative of the sentiment which then prevailed amongst us. I said: " thin Let the Russians come, if they please. They will find behind the serried ranks of one of the finest armies in the world the multitudinous races and peoples of India, united as one man, resolved to die in the defence of their hearths and their homes, and for the maintenance of the honour and dignity of the Empire." Such was the feeling in 1885; such would substantially be the feeling now if there was a repetition of the Pendjeh incident. But it will be said: "Oh! there are the anarchists, and there have been anarchical developments in Bengal." I desire to repeat what I have said more than once here and in my own country—and I re-echo the sentiments of the vast majority of my countrymen—that we deplore these anarchical incidents and have condemned them with the utmost emphasis. The mind, the judgment, the conscience of the country are arrayed against them. I regard them as a passing phase of excitement which will disappear under the soothing effects of progressive and conciliatory measures.

May I pause for a moment to enquire into the secret of that wonderful loyalty and devotion of the Colonies to the Empire, which is one of the most pleasing features of the Imperial system ? The secret is told in one word—it is self-government. Self-government is the cement of the Empire ; it is not inconsistent with the paramountcy of British rule in India. On the contrary, in my opinion, and in that of my countrymen, self-government will make that rule permanent—it will broadbase the Empire of the King on the gratitude, the contentment, and the affections of a vast and multitudinous people. India wants self-government suitable to the development of the ideals that have grown up under the fostering care of the British people. That is our first and last request. And is there any Britisher here or outside these walls—and in the term Britisher I include his kinsmen over the seas—who will not sympathise with an appeal which is in such entire consonance with his own instincts, with the justice of the case, with the orderings of Divine Providence, who has assigned to each nation in the grand and progressive evolution of affairs the full, the free, the absolute, the unfettered control of its own destinies ? India in the enjoyment of the blessing of self-government—India prosperous, contented, and happy—will be the most valuable asset of the Empire, the strongest bulwark of Imperial unity. And the Empire thus knit together upon the basis of common civic rights and obligations may bid defiance to the most powerful combination that may be formed against it and may gaze with serenity and confidence upon the vicissitudes which, as all history tells us, have wrecked the fortunes of States and thrones which relied upon the security of physical force rather than upon the paramountcy of those moral laws which represent the index-finger of Divine Providence in the dispensation of human affairs. (Loud applause.)

AT THE INDIANS' DINNER IN LONDON

Mr. Surendranath Banerjea was entertained at dinner by the Indian residents in London a the Westminster Palace Hotel.

The usual loyal toasts having been duly honoured, the toast was drunk with the utmost enthusiasm amid loud cries of "Bande Mataram" when Mr. Surendranath Banerjea said:

There are moments in the lifetime of an individual when he may truly call himself happy. One of those moments has sounded for me now, when I find gathered together in this hall representatives of the culture, the civilisation, the wealth and the intellect of India, associated with you, Sir, to welcome me on my coming to this country. (Cheers.) It is an index of the growing feeling of solidarity between the different races and peoples of India upon which the best prospects of Indian regeneration so largely depend. (Cheers.) May this feeling grow and deepen to the lasting glory of the Motherland and the credit of English rule in India. (Cheers.) To-day I find myself away from home, but yet in a second home surrounded by the loving kindness of friends who, like yourselves, have adopted me into the bosom of your little community. Your kindness and hospitality are worthy of the best traditions of our people, and they will be a stimulus and incentive to those who, like myself, seek to tread in the difficult, and, in these days, somewhat thorny and dangerous paths of public life in India. Next to the approbation of his own conscience, the highest reward to which a public man aspires is the applause of his fellow-countrymen. (Cheers.) This function to-day affords overwhelming evidence that I possess, may I say in unstinted measure, your support of my public conduct. (Cheers.) I am not so foolish as to imagine that that approbation extends to every item of my public life. I am not so foolish as to imagine that I, or anybody else, can claim to be infallible, for I recognise the truth that infallibility is the prerogative and monopoly of the Government—(laughter)—which possesses another gift of equal value—the knack of never confessing to a mistake or amending it, but regarding it as a settled fact. I do not claim from you a special certificate of approval covering the whole of my public life. I know that in respect of public matters there will always be differences of opinion. Uniformity in my judgment, and I think in the judgment of most public men, means stagnation. Rational differences of opinion conceived in a spirit of liberality, and expressed in the language of moderation, are the unerring indices of the growth of a healthy public life. Charity amid differences, self-restraint amid the most enthusiastic outbursts of patriotic fervour, regard for the law and the Constitution—in respect of which I think the Government might set an example by not enforcing a lawless law and deporting Indians without trial—and, above all, sacred concern for the Motherland and a firm and unflinching determination to spend and be spent in her service, these, in my judgment, constitute the principles of Indian public life as I understand them to-day. (Cheers.)

AT THE INDIANS' DINNER IN LONDON

You have aksed me to discuss the problems of India—complicated and multiform problems, such as they present themselves to us to-day. I confess I find myself in a position of some little difficulty and embarrassment. A spectator sees more of the game than the actual players. I am not a spectator: I am in the thick of the fight. (Cheers.) I may claim to be in the front rank of battle surrounded by gifted self-sacrificing comrades in arms, some of whom, alas, have been deported without trial, and some of whom I would have liked to bring over to this country as samples of the race among whom a policy of repression has been introduced, and who in some quarters are considered unfit for self-government. It has often struck me that it would be a most useful thing—beneficial to England and to India alike—if we had in this country a Session of the Indian National Congress—(hear)—and this impression has been accentuated by my experience in connexion with the Imperial Press Conference. A Session of the Indian National Congress in London would be an object-lesson the significance of which it would be difficult to exaggerate. We have been declared to be unfit for self-government. Let us come face to face with the British public and let them see and decide whether the people of our great and ancient land are unfit for the inestimable boon. (Cheers.)

Naturally enough, on an occasion like this, you wish for first hand information. We have suffered from sensational journalism : we have been the victims of grotesque exaggeration. I myself was declared to have been crowned King of India—(cheers and laughter)—to have become a rival and competitor of his Gracious Majesty Edward VII, to whom we all owe honour and allegiance. A little incident took place the other day to which I desire to call the attention of this gathering. At Manchester a large number of my countrymen did me the honour of waiting upon me with a garland, which they presented to me. There was present on that occasion the representative of one of these sensational journals which shall be nameless—(Name! name! and cries of "Daily Mail.") I am not going to disclose the secrets of my prison-house. I approached him and I said: "This is what you once declared to be the 'crowning of Emperor Banerjea'." He denied the impeachment, and the matter ended. It seems to me it would be most desirable to organise a system by which cable reports could be sent to this country which would neither exaggerate nor extenuate, but simply tell the truth, the whole truth, and nothing but the truth. (Hear, hear.) I appeal to my fellow-countrymen and to our English sympathisers, to whom we are beholden for their very disinterested services, to interest themselves in forming an organisation of this kind in order to put an end to the mendacity of which we have in the past been innocent victims. (Hear.) I will not dwell further upon these considerations.

I will plunge into the subjects to which you have called my attention. You have referred to Lord Morley's scheme of reform. We welcomed it with gratitude and enthusiasm. But it is not correct to say that it outstripped our anticipations. In one respect at least it fell short of our hopes—of what, indeed, we had reason to expect. We wanted the power of the purse. (Cheers.) It does not give us the power of the purse. You, Sir, have laid stress upon the financial drain from India. Yes, if the economic condition of India is to be raised, if the incessant outflow for Home Charges is to be stopped, if the raiyat is to be reclaimed from the depth of misery and poverty into which he has fallen, the people must be largely associated with their rulers in the financial control of India. Am I to understand that in the long and illustrious muster roll of distinguished Indians we have not at the present moment fit successors to Todar Mall and Bir Bal and Salar Jung and Madhava Rao? (Cheers.) If an admission to that effect is to be made it implies a monstrous reflection on British rule. It means that after two centuries under the most civilised administration on earth, the Indian people have become so demoralised, so emasculated, so utterly wanting in intellectual power and virility, that they are not able to come up to the standard of their fathers. I will not myself make such a charge. I will not permit anyone in this room to make such an outrageous charge against the civilised administration which presides over the destinies of our country. We have the men, but our rulers will not look at them : they will not select them : they will not trust them. That is the charge which I wish to bring against the Government : not that it has demoralised us or rendered us a race of imbeciles, but that it is so absorbed in the pursuit of interests peculiar to itself that it will not take a broad view of the situation and associate the people in the task of administration. If it could do that, if it could rise to the height of its responsibilities, a distinct step would be taken for the economic improvement of the condition of our people.

But I have been straying very far from the point I was discussing. Under Lord Morley's scheme of reform, we have not got all we wanted. But still it is right and proper that we should do justice, and, therefore, we are bound to admit that the scheme represents a distinct advance upon the existing methods of administration, and that in its culmination it will give us a real and effective measure of self-government. There is growth in all institutions. No Government can enact a measure—be it good, or be it bad—which is not at once subjected to a process of transformation, slow but steady, under the operation of those immutable moral laws which form a part of the eternal order of things. Forces gather around it which give it an impulse and direction that often lead to great and unexpected results. What a vast difference there is between the Parliament of Simon de Montfort and the great assembly which now controls the destinies of so vast a section of the human race. There is a growth in all things, and we believe there will be a growth in connexion with the institutions which Lord Morley is going to establish. We therefore accept them as a beginning pregnant with immense potentialities. (Cheers.) In that spirit and in that sense we welcome the scheme with enthusiasm and with gratitude. (Hear.) That is the position of educated Bengal—I may say of educated India—with regard to Lord Morley's reforms. But there is a rift in the lute. The enthusiasm—the tremendous outburst of enthusiasm—which the scheme evoked has been chilled by an unhappy pronouncement made by Lord Morley—a pronouncement to the effect that he will be no party to the reversal of the partition of Bengal. You, Sir, did not honour Bengal in your address by the mention of her great fundamental grievance. The partition is our greatest grievance, and it is the root-cause of the prevailing discontent. (Hear.) Of Lord Morley I desire to speak with the utmost possible respect, and I think my feelings are shared by a large body of my fellow-countrymen.

We have sat at his feet—I have done so, at any rate—and we have gathered from him lessons of political wisdom. When Lord Morley says that he will be no party to the reversal of the partition of Bengal, I venture to hope that that pronouncement does not preclude him from considering proposals, not perhaps for the reversal, but for the modification of the partition. I venture to hope that the illustrious author of "Compromise" will apply that policy to the great grievance of Bengal. If anybody were to tell me that there was no hope for a modification of the partition, I would tell him in reply that there was no hope for the conciliation of Bengal. The co-operation of the people in the working of the Reform scheme is essential. Is it possible to ensure the success of any administrative measure, however hopeful or promising it may be, without the willing concurrence and the hearty co-operation of the people concerned? We have only to look to the dead failure of the Calcutta Municipal Act for an illustration of that. (Cheers.) My friend Mr. Cotton over there cheers that statement. He knows something about the Calcutta Municipal Act. In 1899, under Lord Curzon's administration, the Corporation of Calcutta—an institution of local self-government—was officialised. The proportion of elected members was reduced from two-thirds to one-half. We prayed and begged and entreated, and exhausted all the resources of constitutional agitation. But it was all in vain. Lord Curzon had made up his mind, and there was nobody to bring him to book, and, as a final protest against the officialisation of the Corporation, 28 Commissioners, including your humble servant, tendered their resignations. The people took their cue from us, and stood aloof from the administration. They displayed towards it the greater distrust. What has been the result? Despite the most strenuous official white-washing—and Indian officials are past masters in that art—I exclude ex-officials, of course—(a laugh)—despite the most strenuous official white-washing, we find that the Calcutta Municipality has been pronounced to be a failure, and the Decentralisation Commission has recommended a revision of its constitution on the lines of that of the Bombay Corporation. (Cheers.) Lord Morley has declared the partition of Bengal to be a settled fact, but this statement is coupled with an admission which makes it absolutely untenable, for Lord Morley says that there were errors in the original scheme, but that on the whole it was as good a scheme as could have been conceived. And he added that it was a mere question of boundaries.

If these things are admitted, then why should the partition be regarded as a settled fact? (Hear, hear.) Is it logical in the face of these admissions to consider the partition a settled fact? Statesmen, I know, are not bound to be logical, but they are, at any rate, bound to be just and reasonable, and they ought not to over-ride paramount claims. If it is admitted there were errors in the original plan of partition is it fair to perpetuate them in the permanent administration—an arrangement affecting the happiness of millions of people—is it fair to stereotype a blunder which must be disastrous to the credit of the administration ? I can think of nothing more calculated to shock popular confidence in the integrity and sense of fairness of the British Government than for it to say, "We have committed a blunder, but refuse to redress it" That is the dictum of absolute and autocratic power and not the reasoned judgment of responsible statesmanship. (Hear.) But I will say this. From the point of view of the administrator, although not from the point of view of the sentimentalist and of the philosopher, the partition has been a great blunder; it is the root-cause of the present discontent. (Cheers.) Here, fortunately, I am supported indirectly by valuable official testimony. Of course there is no direct official testimony. Officials never do confess to a mistake. But there is a body of corroborative evidence, the value of which Mr. Mackarness—(cheers)—will recognise. You will all remember the case of the Alipur Bomb prisoners.

They were charged with conspiring against His Majesty the King-Emperor. The date in the indictment is fixed at or about October 16, 1905. I ask you to bear that date in mind. It is very important. (Hear.) October 16, 1905, was the date of the partition of Bengal, and therefore we have in this official statement, which is part of a pure judicial proceeding submitted on the responsibility of the Crown—a suggestion to the effect that the partition was the *fons et origo* of all the discontent and troubles that have followed. Furthermore, the partition has brought about, I am sorry to say, a strong alienation of feeling between Hindus and Mahomedans in some parts of the country leading to riots, disturbances, and breaches of the peace. The policy of dividing Bengal may be acceptable to a few, but it is the instrument of the weak. It is a prolific source of embarrassment. We in Bengal cannot accept the partition as a settled fact. (Hear, hear.) We decline to do so. (Cheers.) And appeal to you here to sympathise with us in the great struggle in which we are now engaged. I tell you that that struggle will continue so long as the partition is not modified. The agitation will continue, the excitement will grow, the tension will increase, and I ask you, is all this conducive to good government? Let the Government pause and consider. Our responsibility is over. The responsibility now must rest upon our rulers and administrators. We have raised our warning voice.

I will not trouble you further with this question of the partition. I am afraid I have already taken too much time with that. (Cries of "No.") You have referred to the imprisonment of the editors. Do you know as a little historical fact that I was one of the first Indian editors to be imprisoned? I am in the deepest sympathy with my comrades in distress—I think it is monstrous that punishments of the magnitude of those which have been imposed should have been inflicted upon them. I hope and trust that a general order of amnesty will soon be issued, and that these men will be released. I fear that the official authorities lose their balance of mind when they come to deal with cases of this kind. It is natural, perhaps, for them to be panic-stricken, and I sympathise with them to a certain extent; but at the same time I believe they ought to be above all such distemper of mind. (Cheers.) Reference has been made to the domiciliary visits which have become so frequent of late. I have personally enquired into this matter, and I am prepared with some first-hand information with regard to it. The news I have at the present moment is about two weeks old. Two hundred young men are treated as suspects, their houses are visited night after night by the police. I think it is a great shame. (Cheers.) No charges have been made against them; they certainly have not been convicted of any. It is upon the secret reports of a secret police—the most unscrupulous in the world—that these young men have been subjected to the degradation and annoyance of police surveillance. The secret police in India are the most unscrupulous in the world. I think they might give points to the Russian police in their amazing facility of fabricating evidence. (Hear, hear.) I think that public opinion in this country ought to be brought to bear on this matter. (Cheers.) I would appeal to our English friends here to interest themselves in it, and to try to put an end to a scandal which is deepening the discontent in the new province. (Hear, hear.)

I pass now to the question of the deportations. Speaking as an Indian, it would be impossible for me to allude to this question without expressing our deep gratitude—the deep gratitude of all Indians—to Mr. Mackarness and his colleagues, including Sir Henry Cotton, Mr Swift MacNeill, Mr. Keir Hardie, and, last but not least, that devoted worker for the cause of India, Dr. Rutherford,—(cheers)—for the action they have taken in the House of Commons on this question. It is impossible for me to exhaust the list of gentlemen who have thus assisted us, but their services will remain enshrined in the grateful recollection of my countrymen, and they will be remembered as the friends who stood by us in the hour of darkest need. (Cheers.) It has been sought to justify these deportations, and that by no less an authority than the Prime Minister himself, on the ground that they have contributed to abate the elements of mischief which were in full operation at the time the deportations took place. I respectfully but most emphatically dissent from this view—(cheers)—and I am about to submit for your consideration certain facts which I think will bear out my contention. These deportations took place on December 11, 1908—I think it was a Friday. Since then there have been three cases of bomb-throwing at passing trains, and since then too my esteemed and dearly beloved friend Babu Ashutosh Biswas, the Public Prosecutor of Alipur, has been murdered within the precincts of the court. How, then, is the Prime Minister justified in saying that these elements of mischief have been abated and that that result has been brought about by the deportations ? To connect the bomb-throwing, even by implication, with some of the men deported constitutes in my judgment a foul libel on them. (Loud cheers.) Babu Krishna Kumar Mitra and Babu Aswini Kumar Dutt and many others are men of whom, in my opinion, we may well be proud. (Cheers.) Religious, God-fearing, scrupulously honest and scrupulously constitutional in their methods of public work, their deportation has created a sense of profound sorrow and indignation throughout the length and breadth not only of Bengal but of India. It is remarkable that in the discussions and controversies which have raged round this question not a single word has been said about the success or otherwise of similar measures that were taken in 1907 in the Punjab. Why this silence? It is very significant, and in my opinion it involves a confession of the failure of deportation as an instrument for the suppression of crime. The Punjab has been pacified. Was it due to the deportations or even to the prolonged agony of the Rawalpindi trial ? My answer is an emphatic "No." It was the vetoing of the Colonisation Bill by Lord Minto-(cheers) —which brought back peace and tranquillity to that distracted province. Let the same policy be adopted in Bengal and the same results will follow. Let the partition be modified, and there will be such an outburst of enthusiasm as will wipe out the recollection of bitter memories of the past. (Hear, hear.)

It has been said again, in justification of these deportations, that there was terrorism in India, that it was difficult to procure evidence, and that the ordinary processes of law had proved inadequate. Terrorism by whom? Was it by the people or by the police? Was it terrorism by the people or by the magistracy? I say the terrorism was by the police and by the magistracy, and Chief Justice Jenkins shall be my witness. (Cheers.) In the notorious Midnapur case information was given against 154 persons as having entered into a plot for murdering British officials in the Midnapur district. Thirty persons were arrested, including the Raja of Narajole, who had a great stake in the country, and to whom the Government itself had done honour by conferring on him titular distinction. Thirty persons, including the Raja, were condemned to solitary confinement in cells reserved for convicts and murderers. (Shame.) This went on for six months. There was a tremendous outcry, and the Press expressed itself in language of warmest condemnation and indignation. The Advocate-General, Mr. Sinha, now Law Member of the Viceroy's Council, who is worthy of all honour—(cheers)—was deputed by the Government of Bengal to investigate this matter, and having gone through the papers he recommended that 27 out of the 30 prisoners should be discharged. They were accordingly released. The three others were sent for trial; their case came before the Sessions Judge, and they were convicted as a matter of course—(laughter)—and sentenced to transporation for long terms. An appeal was filed, Chief Justice Jenkins and Mr. Justice Mookerjee heard it, and they delivered a scathing judgment condemning the tactics of the police and the magistracy alike. In that judgment Chief Justice Jenkins said that Mr, Weston, the Magistrate of Midnapur, who was in charge of the prosecution, caused the arrest of the father of one of the prisoners with a view to obtain, to extract, to extort—whichever term you please—a confession from the son. (Cries of "Shame.") I think it is a matter of unutterable shame.

Let us pass from the magistrates to the police. The Chief Justice says the court accepts the theory of the defence that a bomb had been put into the house of one of the accused by the police with a view to fabricating evidence! Gentlemen, I put it to you to say whether this is terrorism by the people or terrorism by the police and the magistracy. (Cheers.) Then we were told that the ordinary processes of law had proved inadequate. I was under the impression that the Executive had been strengthened, and that enormous powers had been given to it by special legislation. Are we to understand that that special legislation was of no use, so that it had to be supplemented by powers of deportation? Never was there a confession of more hopeless failure. (Loud cheers.) Where in the history of the world has repression ever been successful? It paralyses healthy and useful activity; its arm is never long enough to reach the secret dens of secret societies which are fostered and brought into being by repressive methods.

Personal liberty is the indefeasible right of British subjects, no matter in what part of the world they may be born. In the days of negro slavery the shackles of the negro burst from around him the moment he touched the consecrated soil of Britain. Are we to understand—I am talking as a Native of India—that these golden traditions have been forgotten or that they are to be held to be inapplicable to the

Indian subjects of His Majesty? To us these deportations have been a matter of the deepest disappointment. We had regarded the Liberal Party as the guardians of popular freedom and as the champions of Indian popular rights. (Cheers.) But when we see it enforcing against us antiquated and obsolete enactments of this kind, deporting our best men without trial, the shock communicated to our feelings has an intensity which it is impossible for me to describe. (Cheers.) But that is the position of affairs. It is for us, my Indian friends, to face it with firmness and at the same time with moderation and self-restraint—to keep in check the elements of lawlessness and to adhere with scrupulous fidelity to constitutional methods of agitation. We have worked hard up till now with inadequate results. The journey may seem long and wearisome: the promised land may appear to be distant, but uplifted by hope and by faith—an undying faith in the high destinies of our country—let us fight the good fight, and I am confident that the God of all nations will vouchsafe us the victory—that victory which awaits those who, inspired by sublime confidence in His dispensation and in the paramountcy of the moral laws, seek to work out the regeneration of the country in a spirit of peace, of righteousness, and absolute self-consecration. I will say no more. I thank you most heartily for the kind attention with which you have listened to what I have said. I hope and trust that in the future that is before us united brotherhood, enthusiasm, public spirit and self-dedication may be the watchwords of the great Indian people ; that the country will be restored to the glories of ancient times, and that once again it will become one of the greatest nations in the world. In that hope, in that belief and conviction let us work, and success will attend our efforts. (Loud and long continued cheering.)

AT SIR W. WEDDERBURN'S BREAKFAST

At the invitation of Sir William Wedderburn, a number of Members of Parliament and others interested in Indian affairs met on Tuesday (June 29) at the Westminster Palace Hotel, to welcome Mr. Surendranath Banerjea on his visit to England as a delegate to the Imperial Press Conference. Sir William was in the chair, having on his immediate right the principal guest, and on his left the Rt. Hon. Sir Charles Dilke, M. P.

SIR WILLIAM WEDDERBURN, rising to welcome Mr. Banerjea, said: Gentlemen, our guest, Mr. Surendranath Banerjea, is a many-sided man—a journalist, an educationist, and a political agitator. But this morning we welcome him specially as a personal friend, one whom we have known and admired for many years. I have said he is a many-sided man. As editor of the "Bengalee" he is recognised as a trustworthy journalist; as founder and head of the Ripon College he is appreciated as a brilliant educationist. But, perhaps, I may say a word regarding him as a political agitator. Some people regard all agitators as mischievous persons. But that is too wide a generalisation. They should remember the angel at the Pool of Bethesda. He was an agitator, he troubled the waters, but the result was good, not bad; the result was the healing of the sick. Such an agitator is our friend Mr. Surendranath Banerjea. His mission is one of healing, to promote peace and goodwill between India and England. At this moment his special desire is to see the full success of Lord Morley's noble scheme of reform and conciliation. But he cannot shut his eyes to the obstacles which stand in the way. These obstacles can be described in two words —Partition and Deportation. To remove these obstacles no Act of Parliament is required, only a stroke of the pen by His Majesty's principal Secretary of State for India. Lord Morley has told us that he does not think well of partition, and the deportations are not any more to his taste. Why should he not accept the assurances and grant the prayer of Mr. Banerjea and his friends, the Indian Constitutional Party, who are intimately acquainted with the facts, and whose aims and interests are identical with our own ? Indians know best where the shoe pinches, and they can tell us how to make India contented and prosperous. In asking this goodly company to extend a very hearty welcome to our distinguished guest, I will call on Mr. Allan Hume to say a few words. Mr. Hume was the founder of the Indian National Congress, and can tell us how Mr. Surendranath Banerjea, with the Congress, and before the Congress existed, has given his whole life's work to the cause of the Indian people. After Mr. Hume's high tribute to Mr. Banerjea about his many-sided activities in the cause of India and her people,

Mr. SURENDRANATH BANERJEA, who was loudly cheered, said : I thank you very heartily for the warm welcome, the truly English welcome, which you have extended to me, and I thank you, Sir William Wedderburn, and you, Mr. Hume, for the kind words in which you have couched that welcome. I cannot persuade myself for one moment that I deserve the very kind things which you have both said of me. (Cries of "Yes.") I ascribe them to the partiality, friendship, and affection which you naturally feel for one who has been associated with you for so many long years in the trying, difficult, and arduous work of uplifting the political status of my countrymen. (Cheers.) I am here to-day not as an educationalist, not even as a journalist, but as a public agitator. (Cheers.) I am proud of the title of public agitator. I am not a public agitator in the sense of one who seeks to stir up strife, but I am one in the sense of one whose whole mission is that of a peacemaker. (Hear, hear.) You, Sir, have observed that I am for peace. I have always been for peace, and for a period extending over the lifetime of a generation I have tried in my own humble way, according to my lights and according to my opportunities, to serve my King and my country. It has been the chief aim of my public labours to establish peace—peace as between the Government and the people, peace as between Hindus and Mahomedans, peace as between rival sects and creeds—and thus to broad-base the Empire of His Majesty on the goodwill, contentment, and affectionate gratitude of the vast population committed to his charge. (Cheers.) If you will permit me to make a personal reference, I will say that I was one of the first to welcome Lord Morley's scheme of reform. I was associated with a distinguished body of representative men who, as a deputation, waited upon His Excellency the Viceroy in order to congratulate the Government upon that scheme of reform. (Hear.) Speaking for my educated countrymen, I will say that we are anxious and eagerly solicitous for the success of that reform scheme, because we recognise the fact that with it are bound up the hopes for the future self-government of India. (Cheers.) But at the same time we cannot shut our eyes to the difficulties which have been created by the Government itself, and, I am sorry to say, also by Lord Morley himself.

I feel that I owe it as a duty to my country and to the Government to point out the risk, the imminent, serious risk, as I believe of the failure of that scheme in Bengal if the partition is allowed to remain unmodified. "The partition!"—I am almost tired of repeating it, but I intend to continue to repeat it—the agitation against the partition must continue until the partition has been withdrawn or modified. (Cheers.) The partition is our chief grievance. It is the root-cause of the present unrest. If anybody were to tell me, no matter how high and exalted his position, that there is no hope for the modification of the partition, I would say to him in reply that there is no hope for the conciliation of Bengal, or for securing the hearty co-operation of the people in the working of the reform scheme. (Hear.) If Lord Morley were to hold out in his right hand the gift of the reform scheme and in his left the gift of the modification of the partition, and were to tell the people of Bengal "You cannot have both, make your choice," my country would with overwhelming spontaneity declare themselves in favour of the modification of the partition, and would allow the reforms to come in their own good time. (Cheers.) I know it is said that this grievance is only a sentimental one. Be it so ; a sentimental grievance is a grievance that is felt. (Hear.) I believe that if any part of England, say one of the Northern Counties, were cut aloof from England and incorporated with Scotland, and formed into a separate administrative area, there would be such a storm of indignation as would sweep away from office the strongest Ministry that has ever been installed at Whitehall. (Hear, hear.) A high Anglo-Indian official—one of the highest—said to me the other day, " Mr. Banerjea, if my country were broken up in the way your province has been broken up, my feelings would be precisely the same as yours." No administration worth the name can overlook sentimental considerations, and such considerations are of special importance in the government of oriental nations, with their imaginative temperaments and their warm susceptibilities. (Hear.)

The greatest Anglo-Indian authorities have condemned this partition. Is there anyone entitled to speak with greater authority upon any Indian question than Lord Ripon ?—(cheers)—the venerable patriarch of the Liberal Party, whose name is enshrined in the grateful recollection of the people of India by reason of the justice, the reason, and the liberality of the measures for which he was responsible while Viceroy of India. (Loud cheers.) Lord Ripon, in an interview which he granted to Mr. Stead recently, said he thoroughly disapproved of the partition. I believe he used even stronger language, and he gave as a reason for his disapproval that it had caused widespread discontent among a population notoriously loyal to the British Government. Lord MacDonnell has declared it to be the gravest blunder ever committed under British rule, and I believe if the sense of the Anglo-Indian administrators of to-day were taken on this point they would be found to heartily endorse that view. (Cheers.) Why, even the authorities who fathered this project seem to be thoroughly ashamed of their progeny, for only the other day they vied with each other in disowning this child of their administrative genius. (Cheers and laughter.)

Could there be a stronger condemnation of the measure than this? Lord Morley said the other day, in a speech in the House of

Lords, that the sentiment against the partition was on the wane. But that is always the official version of a public agitation. Have you ever heard of an agitation in the time of its greatest intensity which has not been described by the officials as dying out ? It is either an artificial agitation manufactured by wire-pullers, or it is a moribund agitation on its last legs. (Cheers and laughter.) With all respect for Lord Morley, I venture to make this submission, that if this proposition were examined in the light of his own previous statements it would be found to be absolutely untenable. In 1906 Mr. Morley declared from his place in the House of Commons that the partition went wholly and decisively against the wishes of the majority of the people concerned.

That was said in 1906. What has happened since that date to reconcile the people of Bengal to that partition ? I will tell you of some of the things which have happened. There have been frequent house searches—a proceeding most abhorrent to the Indian mind. If an Englishman's house is his castle, a Hindu's home is his temple, for it is consecrated by the presence of his household gods whom he worships with a fervour and devotion scarcely less earnest and less exuberant than that which the Romans of old accorded to their Lares and Penates. (Cheers.) There have been numerous house-searches. There have been numerous Press prosecutions. There has been Press legislation of an unexceptionally severe kind. There have been domiciliary visits paid by the police, associations have been wiped out of existence by Executive order, and last, but not least, there have been deportations without trial. (Shame.) I put it to you: If when the partition was originally carried out it evoked a considerable measure of dissatisfaction and discontent, does it stand to reason that the subsequent proceedings—the repressive policy of the past twelve months—can have soothed the public sentiment and reconciled the people of Bengal to the partition? No, Sir, the feeling is there—as strong as ever—deep down in the depths of the national heart. There is, indeed, a feeling of growing despair. (Hear.) The people are beginning to say, "What is the good of agitating when the Government will not listen to us?" Inaction in this case does not mean any cessation of feeling. (Hear.) On the contrary it represents a very grave situation; it involves the loss of public confidence in constitutional methods of agitation. (Hear.)

The cry has been raised, "Rally the Moderates." I will say this. I know of no proceeding more fatal to the growth of constitutionalism in Bengal, or more calculated to weaken the influence of the Moderate Party, to which I have the honour to belong, than this persistent refusal on the part of the Government to listen to our representations in regard to a matter in which it is admitted a grave and serious blunder has been committed. (Hear.) We are on the horns of a dilemma. If we agitate—and we know how to agitate, you have had some experience of that in the past, and, if necessary, we can further develop our powers in that direction—(hear)—if we agitate, we are told it is a test and trial of strength between the Government and the people, and that the Government cannot yield. If we do not agitate, we are told that the feeling against the partition is dying out. So we are fairly between the devil and the deep sea. (Cheers and laughter.) Lord Morley admits that a blunder, a serious blunder, has been committed. He has said the scheme was not the best that could have been devised, and that it went wholly and decisively against the wishes of the majority of the people concerned. He has added that it was a mere question of boundaries, and was not sacrosanct. Why, then, in the name of logic and commonsense, should it be regarded as a settled fact ? I know that statesmen are not bound to be logical. (Laughter.) Lord Morley himself is my authority for that, for he has said it in his monumental work on the "Life of Edmund Burke." A statesman need not be logical, but he is bound to be reasonable, and he is bound to be just. He cannot override the paramount claims of right-doing. Righteousness exalteth nations and the rulers of nations ; righteousness is the vital breath of Imperial statesmanship, and, as a distinguished Anglo-Indian administrator once put it, a single act of unrighteousness, or an act felt to be such, is more disastrous to British rule in

India than would be a great reverse sustained on an Asiatic battlefield. (Hear.)

Lord Morley says that the partition is a "settled fact." Is there such a thing as a "settled fact" in politics or in morals, or even in the material world? Change is the order of nature, and progress the dispensation of Divine providence. The entire programme of the Liberal party throughout its long and memorable history has been a programme of change of the unsettlement of existing and settled facts in obedience to the paramount claims of progress. (Cheers.) Let me say for my countrymen that we decline to accept the partition of Bengal as a settled fact. We decline to accept what we feel in our heart of hearts to be a cruel wrong, what is admitted to be a blunder, and what constitutes a deliberate affront on the public sentiment of our country. (Cheers.) We decline to accept that as among the verities of life and administration, and we shall continue this agitation until it is changed. We feel it is a wrong, and we say that that wrong must be undone. It may be that we may not live to witness the consummation of our agitation. It may be that the flag we hold may drop from our sinking hands, but I believe—such is our confidence in the justice and righteousness of our cause—that others will spring up in our places and take up that flag and carry it to a final, complete, and assured victory. It is in that hope and in that confidence that we are working. (Cheers.) May I be permitted to appeal on behalf of my countrymen for the sympathy of the British democracy in the fight in which we are engaged; a fight based on the deepest public sentiment; a fight based upon right and justice. I am certain that under God's blessing, aided by your sympathies and by those moral forces which work so silently and majestically in the bosom of society, and make for progress aud right-doing—I am certain we shall win this fight. (Cheers.) At any rate, we mean to continue it until we win. (Cheers.)

I am afraid I have taken up too much of your time. (Cries of "No, no.") I wish to say a word or two, and it will only be a word or two, on the question of the deportations. Regulation 3 of 1818 is a menace to our liberties and to the development of that constitutional freedom which is the goal of our political aspirations. (Cheers.) There is a fight at the present moment going on ; a fight that will increase in volume and in intensity between the bureaucracy, who are anxious to retain power, and the representatives of the people, eager to wrest it from the bureaucracy and to hold it in trust for the people. Popular representatives are bound to be in the bad books of the bureaucracy. Their high character, their eminent public service, the confidence and love of their countrymen will not suffice to protect them in times of excitement. They may scrupulously follow the law, but there is a power above and beyond the law. There is this lawless law, Regulation 3 of 1818, which may be put into operation at any moment, and deprive them of their liberty. Men like Babu Krishna Kumar Mitra and Babu Aswini Kumar Dutt are safeguarded by the loyal devotion and affectionate regard of their countrymen, but they have been deported without trial. Babu Krishna Kumar Mitra twice wrote to the Government enquiring what were the charges brought against him, and praying for an enquiry into them. The Government has not thought fit to reply. (Shame.) He and others like him have been deported upon police reports. The Prime Minister said the other day that they had been deported on reports from various quarters, corroborated in various ways; but this is entirely inconsistent with what Mr. Buchanan said in February last, when he stated that the deportations were based solely on police reports, and upon the report of the Deputy Director of the Criminal Investigation Department and his subordinates, who might be implicitly relied upon. (Laughter.) Chief Justice Jenkins has shown us how far they may be relied upon in his judgment in the Midnapur case. (Hear, hear.) He has charged the police with putting a bomb in the house of one of the accused for the purpose of fabricating evidence. He further charged Mr. Weston, a Civilian of long standing, who was in charge of the prosecution of the accused, with having caused the arrest of a man with a view of extorting a confession from his son. (Shame.)

I will not detain you longer, but I do wish

to say this: Ireland has been pacified, not by repression, but by conciliation. I cannot understand why a different policy should be followed in the case of India. (Cheers.) I know Ireland is not India, but human nature is the same all the world over. The white man and the brown man are equally grateful when a boon is conferred, and equally resentful when an injury is done. To mix up coercion with conciliation is to neutralise the good which conciliation may achieve; the graciousness of the boon is gone and the memory of the sting remains. Therefore, in the name of commonsense, for the credit of British Rule, and for the contentment of the people, I earnestly appeal that these repressive methods may be speedily abolished which have armed an unscrupulous police with dangerous powers and sit like a nightmare on the troubled bosoms of my countrymen. With even greater earnestness and emphasis I plead for a modification of the partition. Do not for one moment accept the official version that the feeling against partition is on the wane. The patient is the best judge of the painfulness of the malady from which he suffers. (Hear.) I am the patient, and my countrymen are the sufferers. In their name and in their behalf I earnestly appeal to you to lend all the influence you possess to secure modification of the partition, and I trust that I shall not appeal in vain. (Loud and prolonged cheers.)

THE WORK BEFORE US

AT THE LONDON INDIAN UNION'S RECEPTION

I accept the title of "The father of unrest in India" which Mr. Mullick has conferred upon me. I am, in no way, ashamed of the part I have played in the development of Indian public life or of the fact that I have communicated to the students the impulses of nationality. Unrest means awakened intelligence and public spirit. All who work for the good of mankind appeal to the young as the most likely to receive their message and I am glad and proud that my teachings are held to have produced a profound influence upon the public mind of Bengal. For this, however, I have in a great measure to thank the authorities who sent me to jail in 1883 and who thereby gave an unparalleled stimulus to the national sentiment (A voice—What about the partition ?) I am not going to forget the partition. That is our greatest grievance, the most serious blunder committed by the Government. I have no hesitation in saying that so long as the partition is not modified, the unrest would continue. The special correspondent of the *Times* in India said, only the day before, that the rest of India did not care two straws for the partition. Here are present this evening the representatives of the whole of India and I appeal to you to say yes or no to that enquiry. (Loud cries; we all sympathise.) Of course, you do; and so does the Indian National Congress. This body, representative of all India, has year after year recorded strong resolutions condemning the partition and recommending its modification. I recognise the fact that I and other popular representatives are going down the vale of years and that the great trust of leading the public mind of India would fall upon those I see before me. It behoves you all to qualify yourselves for that trust by discipline, by right-doing, by self-consecration, by the virtue of self-sacrifice. Above all, you must set your faces resolutely against lawlessness and violence. Within the limits of the law you have the amplest latitude of action and if you skilfully and earnestly use those powers the regeneration of our country is only a question of time. For my part, I have great faith in the destinies of my native land, which I am convinced would again take a proud place among the nations of the East. But all depends upon you and upon those high moral qualities which are so essential to national well-being and greatness.

INDIAN STUDENTS AND THE ASSASSINATIONS

AT THE NEW REFORM CLUB

We have met here to-night under the shadow of what all must feel to be a great public misfortune. (Hear.) We have met here to express our sense of abhorrence and detestation at the foul assassination of Sir Curzon Wyllie and Dr. Lalkaka. I do not know what the motives of the crime were. I do not care to enquire about them. Whether they were personal or otherwise, in your name and on your behalf, as well as on my own behalf, I desire to express our emphatic condemnation of the deed and of the motives which inspired it. (Hear, hear.) We are Orientals wedded to the loftiest traditions of morality. We remember, and we remember with pride, that India has been the home of the highest ethical conceptions ; that she has been the cradle of some of the great religions of the world which have played so prominent a part in determining the character, ideals, and aspirations of so large a section of the human race. (Hear.) According to our ideas murder is murder—(hear)—no matter what may be the determining motive, no matter by what specious plausibilities it may be sought to be justified by any apostle of the new principle of morality. (Cheers.) The dominating principle of all religion is the great truth which the Hindu sage taught 500 years before the birth of Christ, and the moral and ethical domination of that sage's teachings extends to this day over three-quarters of the human race. Our principles, our instincts, our deepest religious convictions are all associated with the maintenance of law and order, and these bright considerations of religion have imposed upon us the obligation to denounce lawlessness and violence. (Cheers.)

A number of resolutions will be submitted to you. One of these records the deliberate conviction of this meeting—and I hope it will be passed unanimously by this meeting—the deliberate conviction that lawlessness and violence are fraught with the deepest peril to the best interests of India. (Hear.) Believe me when I say—and I speak with the authority of a public man naving behind me the experience of a whole lifetime—that lawlessness and violence can do us no good. They are pregnant with mischief. In other countries they have arrested the hand of conciliation and progress: in our own they have formed the supreme justification for repression, a policy which I believe every one in this hall deeply deplores, and which I for one will continue to protest against on every possible occasion. Lawlessness and violence have brought Russia to the brink of ruin. They have interfered with the growth and expansion of Russian liberties, and, as a consequence of the unhappy anarchical developments in the country, we have to-day an emasculated Duma, a very different body from the Duma called into being by the fiat of the Czar: it is the Czar's reply to Russian anarchists. Let us see to it there is no repetition amongst our people of these unhappy developments which for the last few years have marked the evolution of political life in Russia. By the strongest obligations of duty, by the love we bear to our country, by the allegiance which we owe to the laws of God and man, we are called upon to do all that lies in our power to avert a fate so full of awful potentialities. (Cheers.)

I recognise the fact that the evil is a serious one—that the Government alone is not able to cope with it; that the Government in this matter needs the co-operation of the community. I notice with a sense of gratification an appeal made in one of the English newspapers to-day to the Indian leaders to assist the Government in this solemn duty. I may say at once on behalf of the community which I have here the honour to represent, that we desire to return to that appeal a most cordial response. But the Government must strengthen our hands. If the Government will not listen to our representations, if our persistent appeals are brushed aside, as they have been—I was going to say contemptuously—but at any rate brushed aside as unworthy of serious consideration, as in the matter of the modification of the partition of Bengal, what becomes of our influence and of our power to help the Government ? We must have effective power before we can help the Government at all, and I desire to press this consideration upon the mind of Lord Morley and of the British democracy, who, after all, are the uncontrolled masters of our destinies. (Hear.) It is with a feeling of pain—and I am sure you all share that sentiment—that I read some observations which appeared to-day in the newspapers—observations made by the Prime Minister in connexion with this murder. Mr. Asquith is reported to have said that this murder affords startling evidence as to the character of the methods adopted by the conspiracy to which he had occasion to refer in the House of Commons on the occasion of an interpellation addressed to him on the subject.

What is the evidence of this conspiracy ? (A voice : "None at all.") But I remember that when Governments are driven into a tight corner, when they find that they have been guilty of a proceeding which is absolutely unjustifiable, then they fall back upon the expedient of a conspiracy. It has done service in the past : I fear it is destined to do service in the future. Some of you may perhaps be able to recall the events of 1897, when the Natu brothers were deported. Lord George Hamilton, who was then Secretary of State for India, was questioned in the House of Commons on the matter in the same way as the Under Secretary has recently been heckled about the Indian deportees. Lord George Hamilton said, in reply to one of the numerous questions addressed to him, that there was a conspiracy of Poona Brahmins which justified the deportations. It has now been proved conclusively that there never was any such conspiracy—that the thing was a gigantic myth. In connexion with another unhappy incident, which happened only a few months back in relation to a high officer of the Government of India in this country, we were told by the prosecuting counsel that there was a conspiracy. We heard nothing further about that conspiracy. But we do know this : that conspirators never sleep over their projects and that watchful alertness is the creed of the conspirator. I say there is not a tittle of evidence—and I throw out the challenge, let it be accepted by whosoever they please—there is not a tittle of evidence to show that there is any conspiracy at all. If there is I call upon the person who formulates the charge to bring it forward in order that we may criticise it. I say that it is a foul libel on Babu Krishna Kumar Mitra and Babu Aswini Kumar Dutt to suggest that they have ever been guilty of any conspiracy against the British Government. (Cheers.) To me, and I think to you also, it will be a matter of relief, and even of positive pleasure, to pass from these effusions, these almost irresponsible effusions, of the Prime Minister to the attitude and temper of the British democracy, the British public, and the British Press as a whole. Their temper and their attitude has evoked in my mind, and in the mind of my countrymen, the deepest gratitude for the common sense and sobriety of judgment of the great nation which, under the orderings of Providence, rules over the destinies of so many millions of human beings in India.

There is no disposition on the part of the British public, or of the Press—with an exception here and there—to associate this crime, this shocking tragedy, with the Indian community, or even with the students as a class. There is no disposition to interrupt the course of that salutary progressive legislation upon which Lord Morley has embarked. The "Times," which leads the van of public opinion in this matter, in an article which I read with the utmost admiration says that the perpetration of this shocking crime will not, and ought not, to prevent the Government from the steadfast pursuit of those reforms which otherwise it might think advisable. I say we are deeply grateful for this attitude of the Press and of the public, and I am confident that it will have a most salutary effect upon public opinion in India. In this connexion may I put in a plea for those disinterested friends of ours in Parliament who, through good report and through evil report, have strenuously, zealously, and indefatigably been fighting the battles of India? Their utterances are no more responsible for these crimes than were the denunciations of Sir Henry Campbell-Bannerman and Mr. Labouchere for the steadfast determination of the Boers to fight their battle for independence. (Hear.)

We have met here to-night to express our detestation of crime and our sympathy with the families of the deceased. I had not the good fortune of knowing Sir Curzon Wyllie, but all that I have heard in respect of him has been highly to his credit. I regret his death : I regret, too, the death of Dr. Lalkaka : he met his death in the cause of duty when he rushed forward to the rescue of Sir Curzon Wyllie. His memory, and the memory of his noble and grand effort, will for ever remain graven in the hearts of his countrymen. I rejoice that this meeting has been held. I rejoice still more that the young Indian community has taken such a prominent part in organising this meeting. It is well that they have done so—that they have taken the earliest opportunity to condemn this foul crime. My feeling about the students is a very strong one. I have been a teacher myself all my life. No student can be an assassin, no student can have recourse to violence and lawlessness unless and until he ceases to be a student, and I see before me a number of young students. The students of to-day will be the citizens of to-morrow. You, gentlemen, who are now within the sound of my voice will be the future leaders of Indian public opinion. Your education, your opportunities, your contact with the West, fit you for these high responsibilities. Realise then the magnitude of this truth, rise to the height of your mission, qualify yourselves for the arduous duties which will pertain to you as the leaders of public opinion. Qualify yourselves for these duties—the greatest that one can think of on this side of the grave; qualify yourselves by discipline, by right-doing, by self-consecration, by the practice of all those virtues which conduce to individual well-being and national greatness. Righteousness exalteth nations, wrong-doing debases them.

Above all, safeguard yourselves against the snares, the temptations of lawlessness and violence. Remember that at the present moment your countrymen are engaged in a constitutional struggle for constitutional freedom. It is the noblest struggle that can excite enthusiasm in any human being. In that struggle we need the sympathies of Englishmen and of the civilised world, and, above all, the blessing of Almighty God. But you will forfeit them by violence and lawlessness. I have been a teacher myself all my life. Generation after generation of students have sat at my feet and have derived from me the impulses which have become the impulses of their lives. I am therefore entitled to speak to you with some authority. I am entitled to guide, to entreat, if need be to remonstrate, with you. Take it as an injunction from one who through his life has felt the deepest and most affectionate interest in your well-being, take it as an injunction from me that if you wish well for your country, you wish her to be prosperous and brave, create among yourselves a powerful body of public opinion—a strong moral force which shall condemn with unhesitating emphasis all that partakes of lawlessness and violence. By so doing you will erect the most effective barrier against the recurrence of incidents such as the one we have met here to-night to deplore, and then you will have prepared what I conceive to be the royal road to the intellectual, moral, industrial and political regeneration of the great and ancient land to which you and I have the great pride to belong. (Loud cheers.) I have to announce that we have received from the Indian Association of Calcutta, which represents one of the most active organisations we have in Bengal for the propagation of political ideas—an Association with which I happen to be associated as Secretary—a telegram to the effeet that there is a feeling of widespread indignation at the atrocious murder of Sir Curzon Wyllie and Dr. Lalkaka. The Indian students at Edinburgh have also telegraphed their strong sympathy with the objects of this meeting to-night. (Hear.)

THE LIBERAL PARTY'S DUTY TO INDIA

AT THE EIGHTY CLUB

This meeting of the Eighty Club desires to express its profound condolence with the families of Sir Curzon Wyllie and Dr. Lalkaka in the terrible loss they have suffered, and as a mark of sympathy hereby decides to adjourn the discussion.

Mr. SURENDRANATH BANERJEA (who was received with applause) said: I desire thoroughly to associate myself with the vote of condolence, and the proposal for adjourning as a mark of the honoured dead. With your permission I would like to repeat what I have had occasion to say at meetings of my countrymen, that we Indians hold this foul act of assassination in the utmost horror and detestation. (Applause.) I am an Indian. I am proud of my nationality, of the fact that I am the representative of a culture and civilisation that carries the mind back to the dawn of human history. Five hundred years before the birth of Christ a member of my race—Siddhartha—renounced the splendours of royalty, assumed the garb of a hermit, and proclaimed the religion of pity and compassion. This religion of love is our heritage. Our instincts and our traditions, and our deep-seated convictions are all against acts of lawlessness and violence, and you may therefore realise the intensity and the horror, the grief, the indignation which we feel at this atrocious crime.

We make no distinction between murder, the impelling motive of which is gain or simply sordid consideration, and the murder committed in the frenzy of political passion. According to our ideas, though they may appear old-fashioned to the modern school of casuists, murder is murder, no matter what might be the determining motive of the crime, no matter under what pretext it is sought to be justified. I do not stand alone in this conception of the crime which we deplore. I am at this moment voicing the sentiments of my countrymen. There never was a more representative meeting held in London—largely attended by young men—than that which met on Saturday last at the New Reform Club. There was at that meeting representatives of all parties and all religions: there were Hindus and Mahomedans, Parsees and Christians. There were loyalists and ultra loyalists, and there were Moderates and Extremists. All jcined in condemning—unanimously and emphatically condemning—the deed, and repudiating violence as a legitimate weapon.

I confess there may be some terrorists outside our ranks, men who do not belong to any recognised political party. They are a danger to the Government and to the cause of national and constitutional progress; but I venture to hold that their activities cannot put back the even course of Indian politics or the steady movement of Indian public opinion towards peaceful development. I think as I read the Indian problem I may say this: The situation in India is not determined by the mischievous activities of a few fanatics, but by the well-known movements of the great body of the Indian people who are thoroughly loyal to British rule, and who realise the blessings which the British have conferred upon my native land.

I deplore the assassination as a great public misfortune to the people of India. It will enormously weaken our cause, and in the same proportion it will strengthen the hands of our enemies—for we all have enemies—the opponents of Indian political reform, the reform on which Lord Morley has embarked. Take it from me, India is loyal, thoroughly loyal to the British nation, and the constitutional party are in overwhelming majority and these fanatical terrorists represent but a temporary flutter on the calm surface of Indian politics, which should not have the effect of diverging the Government from the pursuit of those reforms with which the happiness of millions of my countrymen are bound up. (Hear, hear.)

To pause, to hesitate, to postpone, would be disastrous to British rule, and would be evidence of weakness which would produce the most painful impression on the public mind of India. The Liberal Party ought to see to it that neither our friends in Parliament nor our friends in Downing Street are hindered in the pursuit of the policy of conciliation with which the happiness of the future is bound up. Conciliation is the remedy to be adopted. The assassination has been a terrible blow at the development of constitutionalism and constitutional liberty in India, and we appeal to you as representatives of the Liberal Party to come to our rescue in this hour of our crisis, and I am sure I do not appeal in vain. (Applause.) I thoroughly associate myself with the resolution which has been proposed. (Applause.)

WHAT INDIA WANTS

AN INTERVIEW WITH MR. STEAD

I travelled down to Lord Northcliffe's seat at Sutton with Mr. Banerjea when the editors of the *Empire* went down to lunch at that delightful place, and formed the highest opinion of his lucid intelligence, his marvellous command of English, and his passionate devotion to his native land. I had the honour of being one of the guests at the banquet given to him by his fellow-countrymen in England at the Westminster Palace Hotel, and was delighted to find in him an orator of brilliant eloquence and a statesman of comprehensive outlook, with a most practical mind. I invited him to my house and there in company with a dozen friends—American, Canadian, Irish and Indian—Mr. Banerjea kindly submitted himself to a process of composite interviewing the gist of which the readers will find condensed in this article.

Mr. Banerjea has been twice President of the Indian National Congress, he has been once in gaol, he is the editor of the *Bengalee* and his repute is such that he was once said to have been crowned king of Bengal as a protest against the partition. He was the only representative of the Native Indian Press at the Conference, and none of the editors of the *Empire* excelled him in eloquence, energy, geniality, and personal charm.

MESSAGE TO BRITISH PUBLIC

"If you were under sentence of death Mr. Banerjea, and the headman's axe was to fall in two minutes, what is the message which you would wish to address to the British public as the last words you were able to utter on behalf of your motherland ?"

Without a moment's hesitation Mr. Banerjea replied :—

"I would say this : (1) Modify the partition of Bengal ; (2) release the deported patriots and repeal the Act which annuls *Habeas Corpus* in Bengal ; (3) amnesty all the political prisoners ; (4) give the people of India financial control of their own taxes ; and (5) grant India a constitution on the Canadian model. That is what I would say, and having said that, I would go to my doom."

"Good!" said I. "Now let us condescend to particulars. I thought you wanted the repeal of the partition?"

PARTITION

"I wish that repeal were possible, but I recognise that Lord Morley, having been perhaps challenged prematurely for an expression of opinion, took up a stand from which he can hardly now be asked to recede. I am a practical man; I ask for modification, not for repeal."

"But I suppose you want to modify it, lock, stock and barrel?"

"What I would like is to see Bengal placed under one Lieutenant-Governor with an executive council of six, of whom two should be Indians. You will have to come to this, for the new province is at present placed in a position of inequality with the old, having no executive council. The next proposal, and one which commanded from of old time the balance even of official opinion, was to divide Behar from Bengal. The people of Behar are distinct in race and language from the Bengalees. All administrative advantages claimed for the original partition would be secured by this arrangement without offending national sentiment. So long as the Bengalee nation is unnaturally cleft in twain by the sword of Lord Curzon, so long will agitation aud unrest continue."

DEPORTEES

"Now as to the deportees?"

"They ought never to have been deported without charge and without trial. They ought at once to be allowed to return home. I hope that will not be long delayed. They are good men, upright citizens who did not deserve deportation."

"And then ?"

"Then Regulation III of 1818 should be repealed or declared illegal. This regulation, passed by a subordinate legislature, deprives the Bengalee subjects of His Majesty of their inalienable rights as British subjects to the privilege of *Habeas Corpus*. I would like repeal outright, for if we bear the burdens and accept the responsibilities of British subjects we ought to have the privileges of freedom from arbitrary arrest, which no one has denounced more strongly than Lord Morley himself."

"Circumstances alter cases. India is not Ireland; to preach is one thing, to practise is another. Is no compromise possible?"

"As a first step," said Mr. Banerjea, "I would accept Mr. Mackarness's proposal that there should be no arrest without specification of the offence and that every accused person should be brought to trial within three months of his arrest."

"I propose as a compromise," I said, "that in future all Indians deported without charge or without trial should be sent to Great Britain in order that they might be at once elected to the House of Commons as Nationalist M. P.'s for Irish constituencies."

"I fear," said Mr. Banerjea, "that there might be difficulties in the way. But if a working alliance could be made, whereby one Indian Nationalist could be provided with an Irish seat, and the whole Irish party took up the Indian national cause, great things might be achieved."

"To return to your message. Do you want

all the bomb-throwers, political cut-throats, etc., let loose to begin again their seditious practices?"

"There are no such persons in custody. I do not ask for an amnesty for the police who used bombs in a criminal conspiracy in order to ruin innocent men. I only want the political prisoners released. There are about sixty of them, and many of them have been sentenced to monstrous sentences for very venial offences."

Mr. Banerjea then went on to instance Mr. Tilak's sentence.

DUMA FOR INDIA

"Do you want a Duma for India?"

"If you mean an assembly representing all India with financial control over the expenditure of India, I say yes. But I would say first give us autonomous provincial governments, with financial control over certain departments of provincial expenditure. Then build upon these provinicial autonomies a central federal council or assembly. That is what we ask, and that is what sooner or later we mean to have."

So far Mr. Banerjea. That is his programme. And "Surrender Not" is the nearest English equivalent to the pronunciation of his name,

Surendra Nath. I do not think that he is likely to abandon any of the planks in his programme. John Morley, of the "Pall Mall Gazette" and of "The Life of Burke," would probably subscribe to them all. But as for Lord Morley—that is another matter.—*Review of Reviews.*

INDIAN UNREST

HOW IT ORIGINATED AND WHY IT CONTINUES

The present unrest in India may be set down to the following causes :—(1) The utter disregard of Indian public opinion by the Government, of which the most notable illustration was afforded by the partition of Bengal. (2) The creation of racial animosities in at least two of the great provinces in India—the Punjab and East Bengal—by the introduction of racial bias into the administration. (3) The wide divergence between profession and practice on the part of the Government and the non-fulfilment of solemn pledges such as are given in the Queen's Proclamation and the consequent failure to associate the people in the government of the country and to accord to them a recognised status in the administrations. (4) The contemptuous treatment of Indians by

Europeans. (5) The hostile attitude of an influential section of the Anglo-Indian Press (whose views are listened to by the Government with respect) in regard to Indian aspirations and the violent and contemptuous language which often marks its utterances. (6) It may be added that the subsequent repressive measures have greatly intensified the unrest.

As regards the first of the aforesaid points, Lord Curzon's administration afforded the strongest illustration. The one end of Lord Curzon's policy was efficiency of administration to be secured by filling the higher offices with Europeans. Against this policy the Congress of 1904 recorded its protest. It was regarded as the practical reversal of the policy of the Queen's Proclamation. In carrying out his policy of efficiency, Lord Curzon treated Indian public opinion with open and undisguised contempt. On the top of all this came the partition of Bengal. It represents the deepest outrage upon popular sentiments which has been witnessed within the lifetime of this generation. When the partition of Bengal was first proposed, it evoked the strongest opposition from both the

Hindu and the Muhammadan communities concerned.

Instead of modifying or abandoning the project, the Government, in the quiet recesses of the secretariat bureau and unknown to the public, enlarged the scheme, added the whole of North Bengal to the original project and, without giving the public the smallest hint of its proceedings, all on a sudden declared that the partition had been resolved upon. The indignation of the people was roused to fever heat, and an agitation was set up against it such as has never been witnessed. It is with us what Home Rule is with the Irish. We cannot give up the agitation against it.

The partition may be said to be the root-cause; and, as Mr. Gokhale has truly observed, the unrest of Bengal has caused the unrest of all India. There are new facts of the most convincing nature created by the partition of Bengal which call for the reconsideration of this measure. Before the partition was carried out, Hindus and Muhammadans lived in amity and goodwill. Since the partition considerable ill-will has been created between the two communities. The bulk of the inhabitants of the new province are Muhammadans and they have been taught to believe that the province has been created for their special benefit, and that they are a privileged class. The Government made no secret of their intention that they wanted to create a Muhammadan province.

Among the fruits of the partition may be mentioned: (1) The unrest in the new province which has created the unrest in Western Bengal and all over India. (2) The policy of repression which followed the partition and has not yet been abandoned, adopted with a view to put down the unrest. (3) The ill-will between Hindus and Muhammadans, who had hitherto lived in peace and amity, which must be a permanent source of embarrassment to the administration. (4) The class bias which is apparent in the policy and the proceedings of the authorities.

The Queen's Proclamation was issued on the 1st November 1858. The Proclamation had abolished race as the test of qualification for high office. The resolution of May 1904 affirmed that race connotes qualities and that the Imperial service (which is the highest service in India) should be a *corps d' elite* to be filled for the most part by Europeans and that even in the technical branches of the public service, the higher appointments should be their monopoly. It is worthy of note that under the Muhammadan rule, race or religion was no barrier to employment in the highest offices, and that Hindus often filled the most responsible offices in the State.

The contemptuous treatment of Indians by Europeans, and the hostile attitude of a powerful section of the Anglo-Indian Press are matters of public notoriety. Sometime ago the Indian Association of Lahore, in an official letter, called the attention of the Government of the Punjab to certain articles which appeared in the "Civil and Military Gazette" of Lahore, which constituted, to quote the words of the Government letter, "a campaign of calumny against the Indian community in general and the educated class in particular."

The reply of the Government (dated 1st November 1907) was interesting and instructive. It admitted the charges against the "Civil and Military

Gazette," but declined to take any legal proceedings. Yet for offences of the same kind, the editor and the proprietor of the "Punjabee" (an Indian newspaper) were prosecuted by the Government, and sentenced to long terms of imprisonment by the courts of law. The law is thus held in abeyance against Anglo-Indian and Muhammadan writers, indulging in the fiercest racial provocatives. Against Hindu offenders of the same class, its terrors are enforced in all their rigour. Yet the fact remains that the Hindus form the bulk of the population in India.

The present unhappy lawless developments have undoubtedly their roots in the prevailing discontent. When a whole community is discontented and exasperated, it is only natural that some people more excitable than the rest should lose their heads and do foolish and violent things. The anarchic development is only one of the outward manifestations of a serious distemper in the body politic, the causes of which are to be found in the reactionary policy of the last sixteen years and more, and which reached is climax during Lord Curzon's regime.

Lord Morley's reform scheme is a notable and distinct step towards conciliation. India is rapidly advancing; and the reform-scheme represents an effort conceived in the spirit of sympathy and liberality to adapt the administration to the newly developed requirements of the situation. It is altogether a mistake to assume, as the special correspondent of the "Times" does, that the scheme makes concessions that are lavish and unsought for. On the contrary, it does not, in some important matters, come up to our anticipations. We have not got the power of the purse which we wanted, at least in some important departments of the State, and we have not got a definite or effective measure of self-government, which we have been urging from the Congress platform. But it is a beginning, and a good beginning, and our people welcomed it as such. In Bengal, however, there is a serious difficulty. The partition remains unmodified and Lord Morley has told us that he would be no party to the reversal of the partition. What Bengal wants is not the reversal but some modification of the partition.

How deplorable the blunder of the partition has been will appear from the policy of repression that has been followed in order to combat the feeling which the partition has evoked. There could be no stronger condemnation of the partition than the adoption of a policy which is in such entire conflict with British traditions of government. The main features of that policy are: (1) House-searches; (2) domiciliary visits by the police; (3) suppression of societies by executive order; (4) deportations without trial. House-searches are most repugnant to Indian feeling. In one case the High Court granted damages for Rs. 500 to a zemindar whose cutcherry (court-house) had been searched by the Magistrate of Mymensingh.

In by far the majority of cases the searches were fruitless, and only served to create irritation. They have created a sense of uneasiness among the Indian community. At Dacca, the capital of the new province, about 200 young men are treated as suspects, and their houses are visited by the police almost every night. No charges have been brought against them.

The head and front of their offence seems to be that they were members of associations which have since been suppressed by order of the Government, but which were perfectly legal when they were connected with them.

Several associations have been suppressed by executive order, without their being allowed the opportunity of explanation or defence. Among them was the Bandhab Samiti of Barisal in East Bengal which did splendid work during the Barisal famine of 1906-7, and whose objects were : (1) The promotion of indigenous industries; (2) the settlement of disputes by arbitration; (3) the promotion of village sanitation. The suppression of an association like the Bandhab Samiti has naturally created very widespread dissatisfaction. As regards the deportations, Mr. Buchanan said from his place in the House of Commons that they were based "solely" on the report of the police and we know from the judgment of Chief Justice Sir Lawrence Jenkins how unscrupulous the police in Bengal are, and how unsafe it is to accept their statements. In the case which Lala Lajpat Rai brought against the "Englishman" newspaper for stating that he had been deported for tampering with the loyalty of Indian sepoys, the Court held that the statement was "a malicious lie." The defence was that it was substantially the statement made by the Government in Parliament. Damages amounting to £1,000 were awarded to Lala Lajpat Rai. All these repressive measures have intensified the excitement and unrest. To mix up coercion with conciliation is to neutralise the good which conciliation may produce by the unhappy leaven of coercion.

I would suggest the following remedial measures:—(1) That the partition of Bengal should be modified. It is the root-cause of the unrest in Bengal, and, as Mr. Gokhale has observed, the unrest of Bengal means the unrest of all India. I may here point out that the Punjab was tranquillised by the redress of a local grievance—*viz.*, the vetoing of the Colonisation Bill by the Viceroy. (2) That the policy of repression should be abandoned and those who have been deported restored to liberty. The Indian public deplore the recent tragedy but they earnestly hope that it will not prejudicially affect the case of the deportees.

(3) That the Government should observe the most rigid impartiality as between race and race and creed and creed. This has always been the strongest bulwark of British rule in India. Any suspicion on the part of the people that this policy has been departed from, would be a source of serious administrative embarrassments and of deep disappointment to a large class of His Majesty's subjects. (4) That a steady advance should be made towards the fulfilment of the pledges given in the Queen's Proclamation in the matter of the appointment of Indians to offices of trust and responsibility.

Daily Chronicle.

RELIGION AND POLITICS IN INDIA

AT CLAPHAM

Mr. Surendranath Banerjea addressing the men's meeting at Grafton Square Congregational Church, Clapham, said : I have great pleasure at the opportunity of addressing such an audi ence on the Sabbath day and in the temple of their worship. In the mind of the Indian people politics and religion are indissolubly blended. We recognise in the movement of public affairs not merely the principle of expediency but the paramountcy of the moral laws. My first words on this occasion, as on others recently, will be to express, on behalf of my countrymen, our abhorrence of the terrible crime committed in London recently—a crime which has shocked the moral sense of the whole community. Terrorism has no recognised place in the movement of Indian society, the whole trend of which is in the direction of orderly and peaceful progress. What amongst us is the problem of problems, the goal of our aspirations? It is the attainment of self-government—self-government within and not outside the Empire; not separation or disintegration, but complete incorporation in the great federation of free States, which has meant so much for the progress and happiness of the world. It is essential to the permanence of the Empire that self-government should be conceded to all its portions; absolute autocracy could never be more than a temporary makeshift. If you ask me how far the Indian people are capable of self-government, I will remind you that the practice of self-government is the best and the only training for the institution of self-government. I have a deep and abiding faith in the potentialities of my race. In the morning of the world, ages before Rome was built and before the forms of government emerged in Europe, India had its system of village communities, self-contained and self-governing. And I will make a further claim—namely, that India is the cradle of that democratic sentiment which has become enshrined in Parliamentary institutions. According to the Indian proverb, wherever five men are gathered together for a public purpose, there the divine spirit made itself manifest. Is it possible to conceive a nobler spiritualisation of the democratic sentiment than this? And further, we had the beginnings of self-government in British India for a quarter of a century in the local bodies called into being a quarter of a century ago by Lord Ripon, the great Viceroy whose loss both India and England are deploring, and whose memory will remain for ever in the hearts of the Indian people because of the justice, wisdom, and liberality of his rule. At a time when a great tidal wave of progress is sweeping over the whole East, when the peoples of the East are exhibiting a passionate hunger for free institutions, is it possible for the English race to refuse the gift of self-government to India?

THE SITUATION IN INDIA

AT THE CAXTON HALL

A meeting was held on July 13, at the Caxton Hall, Westminster, to hear an address by Mr. Surendranath Banerjea. Sir Charles Dilke, *Bart.*, M.P., presided, and was supported on either side by Mr. Banerjea and Sir Henry Cotton, M.P.

Mr. SURENDRANATH BANERJEA, who was loudly cheered on rising, said : Mr. Chairman, Ladies and Gentlemen,—I desire at the outset to associate myself, and I can also speak on behalf of my countrymen, with the observations which you, Mr. Chairman, have been pleased to make regarding the blessed and time-honoured memory of the late Marquis of Ripon. (Hear, hear.) In the illustrious muster-roll of Indian Viceroys he will take his place amongst the most illustrious. His memory will for ever remain enshrined in the grateful recollections of our people. The rulers of India who cling together in our grateful affections are Bentinck, Canning, and Ripon. (Cheers.) I do not think it necessary to repeat the observations which I have made at other public meetings to express the horror and detestation which we have felt at the terrible tragedy which resulted in the deaths of Sir Curzon Wyllie and Dr. Lalcaca, for Indian public opinion in this country and in the homeland is clear and emphatic with regard to it. (Hear, hear.)

For various reasons, some of them not of the most pleasant character, the Indian problem at the present time looms largely into the public view. Our complaint—I mean the complaint of the people of India—is that so little interest is felt in this country regarding the affairs of that great dependency. (Hear, hear.) The apathy of the British public is one of our greatest grievances, because the fact remains, whoever might be our governors and administrators, the British democracy, the electors of Great Britain and Ireland, are the real rulers of India. (Hear, hear.) To them have been entrusted the destinies of 300,000,000 of my fellow-countrymen, not savages or barbarians, but representatives of a great and ancient culture which carries the mind back to the dawn of human history. (Hear, hear.) How is this awful responsibility discharged? I am reminded in this connexion of an Eastern legend, historical in its character and based upon truth. Mahmoud of Ghazni flourished in the eleventh century of the Christian era. His dominions extended far and wide. There lived in a part of his Empire an elderly woman who had suffered a grievous wrong, for one night she found her house burned down, her goods plundered, and her children massacred. Overwhelmed with the awful calamity, she set out to the capital of the Empire and sought her ruler's presence. She presented herself at the palace gates, was ushered into Mahmoud's presence, and laid her complaint before him. Mahmoud heard her case and its tale of sorrow and wrong, and then he remarked: "Woman, you live in a remote part of my Empire. How can you expect me to extend to you the protection of my power?"

And the woman, with that promptitude of resource which characterises her sex—(laughter)—replied: "Sire, why then do you conquer countries to whose affairs you cannot pay sufficient attention, and for which you cannot hold yourself answerable at the Day of Judgment?" (Applause.)

Ladies and Gentlemen, I have no desire to enforce this lesson in its application to the British democracy, but I say this, and I think with your full concurrence, that the responsibility of these islands as regards their great dependency is not discharged by merely appointing your governors and your administrators and leaving them to the discretion of their own sweet wills. (Hear, hear.) I have no desire to make the smallest reflection upon the men on the spot. (Hear, hear and laughter.) I am sure they do their best according to their lights and opportunities; but, after all, they are human beings, dominated with ideas and sentiments, and it may be with the passion of their prejudices. In the old days of the East India Company a Parliamentary Committee used to be appointed every twenty years to enquire into Indian affairs. The labours of this Committee were favourable alike to England and to India, and I do not understand why this practice should not be revived and the Government thereby exercise a beneficent sway over the people, caring for them and in turn being loved by them. There is nothing to lose but everything to gain by such an enquiry. (Hear, hear.) But Governments are slow to move. They will not prepare the materials or provide the grant for impelling progress without the irresistible pressure of public opinion being brought to bear upon them. (Hear, hear.) Yet this is what will have to be done. (Hear, hear.) I have heard it said that if such an enquiry were to take place the machinery of the Government would be dislocated. Well, all I can say is, I have a far greater faith in the stability of that machinery than apparently have those who work it and are responsible for its efficiency. (Hear, hear and laughter.) And this is justified by the lessons of experience. Only eighteen months ago the Decentralisation Committee was appointed to visit India and travel up and down the country, examining numerous witnesses and instituting the most searching investigation.

Ladies and gentlemen, will you believe it, the Government of India actually survived the catastrophe. (Laughter.) No dislocation nor any disturbance of the existing machinery of the Government took place. There was not the slightest deviation from the normal conditions of the administration of the Government, nor was there any deviation in the uses of Indian life and society. My own belief is that if this Committee were continued and their recommendations followed, the Government of to-day would not have been confronted with excitement and unrest and all the deplorable things which have followed in their train. (Hear, hear.) The Government would have been more in touch with the people. And that brings me to the subject of Indian unrest. What is the cause of that unrest, what are the circumstances contributing to it, and what is the solution of the problem? (Hear, hear.) Ladies and gentlemen, I ask you to bear in mind that we in India are a law-abiding and peaceful people. (Hear, hear.) Our instincts traditions, and deepest religious feelings and affections are intimately bound up in the maintenance of law and order. Our ancestors developed a system of ethics and a code of laws upon that proclamation from on high, "Peace and good will among men," which to-day excite the admiration of mankind and constitute an enduring monument of their devotion to peace. What, then, is it that has plunged a people whose antecedents were such as I have described, so peacefully inclined, so adverse to all forms of excitement, into a vortex of unrest which is unparalleled? Edmund Burke has told us—and his dictum has never been challenged, for the reason that it cannot be challenged—that in all controversies between people and their rulers the presumption is that the rulers are in the wrong and the people in the right. (Hear, hear). I say if the matter of this Indian unrest were carefully examined, and there is no tribunal more qualified for the task than the tribunal of the British public, it would be found that the responsibility for this unrest mainly rests, and I am sorry to have to say it, but say it I must, upon the Government of the country, (Hear, hear.)

I blame no one; I am not here to formulate charges against individuals. Even the most dazzling and brilliant of Viceroys fade out of my recollection before the issues involved. I am here to place the facts before you as they affect my countrymen and to vindicate their character as a peaceful and law abiding people. (Hear, hear.) When you have heard those facts I know you will give your verdict in my favour. (Applause.) I am happy to say from the outset England's great mission in the East was realized by the illustrious founders of the Indian Empire. It was not realized by every one, and certainly not by those who went out to India to make money or die of liver complaint —(laughter)—but it was realized by those great and illustrious men whose genius and statesmanship founded the vast and majestic fabric of the Empire of India. Macaulay, speaking from his place in the House of Commons on the occasion of the Charter Act, used language which I for one have ever read with enthusiasm and gratitude. "It may be said," said Macaulay, "that the public mind in India may so expand under our system that it may outgrow that system, and our subjects trained in Western civilization may pray for Western institutions. I know not whether such a day will come, but if it does come it will be the proudest day in the annals of England." I venture to say that that day has arrived, and great are the responsibilities of England. (Hear, hear and applause.) Lord Metcalfe, the liberator of the Indian Press, used similar language when replying to a deputation which waited upon him. "We are not here," he said, "merely to keep the peace and collect taxes...we are here for a higher and nobler purpose, to pour into the East the knowledge and culture and the civilization of the West." (Hear, hear.) The Earl of Shelburne, the great-grandfather of Lord Lansdowne, who opposed the insertion of Clause 3 into the Indian Councils Bill, said on the occasion of the debate in the House of Lords on the Charter Act of 1833 that their lordships would be remiss in the discharge of their duties if they did not offer to the Indian people ample opportunity for developing the high moral and intellectual qualities with which they had been endowed. These utterances embodied a noble policy, and such a policy pressed steadily into the view of the

Indian Government by the most illustrious of Indian administrators has resulted in higher education being introduced into our midst, the Press liberated, local self-government, and the setting up of councils. But can you tell a people whom you have so liberally educated and plentifully supplied with the environments which stimulate public life that thus far shall they go and no further? (Hear, hear.) Yet that has represented the attitude of Anglo-Indian government for the past twenty years.

There you have the beginning of indian unrest, which has now assumed such vast proportions. Can we overlook the wondrous change which has taken place in Asia; changes have been brought about by the victories of Japan over Russia, which had strengthened the confidence of Asiatics in themselves. (Hear, hear.) We have a mighty wave sweeping over Asia which carries with it high ideals and aspirations. India would be false to herself, her ancient culture which she so largely imbibed, and the education she has received if she did not feel revivified in the example of oriental nations struggling for consideration and self-government. (Hear, hear).

On the top of all this excitement came a period of reaction, in which the legitimate aspirations of the people were ignored and trifled with. The people were counted as nothing, we were counted as nothing, we were good for nothing, and we were to do nothing; everything was to be done for us. The generous policy of Lord Ripon was reversed. Local self-government was modified, and the universities, centres of humane and beneficent influence, were officialised, despite the protests of the people. Then on the top of all came the crowning piece of folly—the partition of Bengal. (Hear, hear).

It is true the situation has been somewhat eased by Lord Morley's reform, but this reform scheme has given rise to some considerable diversity of opinion amongst us. (Hear, hear.) There are those representing a section of Indian opinion who hold that it lacks the essential element of genuine reform; that it will serve no useful purpose, and that whatever merits it might have possessed have disappeard in the recommendation of a system of class legislation. (Hear, hear.) On the other hand, there are those who hold a different view altogether.

They declare that the scheme makes lavish concessions—concessions which were never before thought of, and which represent an entirely new and remarkable departure. As an Indian speaking on behalf of my countrymen, I say at once that I totally dissent from this view. The scheme contains no concessions which have not been sought for. So far from the scheme being lavish, I still say that it does not come up to our expectations in regard to many matters which vitally concern the power of the purse. We want definite control at least over some of the great departments of the State ; over sanitation, education, and the public work department. Are you not aware that hundreds of thousands of my countrymen die every year from preventable diseases, such as malaria and cholera? ("Shameful!") Yes, I think it is very shameful indeed. We have been pressing the importance of the matter upon the Government for years. We have cried aloud, but who will listen to us? (Hear, hear.) If we had some effective control over finance, or at least over sanitary measures to be employed, I am convinced that we could prevent to some extent the appalling rate of mortality which desolates homes in Bengal. (Hear, hear.) The expenditure on education is inadequate. The great bulk of it is not being spent for education at all but upon inspection. (Laughter.) As for elementary education, well, the less said the better. (Hear, hear.) If we had any control over finances in regard to education we should devote the money to a useful and profitable purpose. We want the power of the purse and a definite and effective method of self-government. (Cheers.) This we have not got; all the scheme does is—and let me be perfectly candid in the matter—to provide machinery by which representatives of the people would be in a position to bring to bear upon the Government not a direct influence but an indirect moral pressure. (Hear, hear.)

At the same time we have accepted the scheme as a beginning. We recognise that there is such a thing as the growth of public institutions. (Hear, hear.) You cannot make a law, be it good or bad, which is not at once subject to a process of transformation under the operation of immutable moral laws. These are hopes which have gathered round the scheme. They may be fulfilled, or dark clouds may gather, the force of reaction may be in the ascendant so that these aspirations which we have fondly cherished may fall away like shadows. All the same, we do cherish these hopes, and we pray that they may be realised. (Hear, hear). In Bengal the situation has taken a somewhat strained and difficult aspect. In the firmament of that province there is a cloud which is no bigger than a man's hand, but which threatens to overshadow the beautiful prospect pointed out by Lord Morley's scheme. Lord Morley has recently said that he will be no party to the withdrawal of the partition of Bengal. I hope that that pronouncement does not preclude him from considering proposals for the modification of the partition. (Hear, hear.) If any one were to tell me, no matter how high and exalted might be his position, that there is no hope for the modification of the partition of Bengal, I should venture to tell him, in the name of my countrymen, that then there is no hope for the conciliation of Bengal, or for the co-operation of our people in the working of the reform scheme.

(Applause). This partition is our greatest grievance, and in our judgment it is the root cause of the present discontent in India. (Hear, hear.) When it was first announced it invoked the united opposition of the Hindus and the Mahomedans alike. The opposition was so wide spread and so intense that it would have sealed the fate of any measure in this country. But the methods of the Government in India are different from the methods of the Government in England. (Hear, hear.) For this opposition the Indian Government had its revenge. A wider scheme of partition was announced, which had been deliberated on in the secret recesses of the Secretarial Bureau. It was resolved upon in secret and fell like a bolt from the blue upon the astonished people of India. It gave rise to an agitation the parallel of which I have never before witnessed. (Hear, hear.) It is four years since the partition was accomplished, but the wound to-day is as fresh as if it were only inflicted yesterday. (Hear, hear.) There are those who say that the feeling against the partition is on the wane, but we are in the position of unfortunate beings suffering from a painful disease. It has its moments of cessation, but the patient knows no rest or peace so long as the root cause of the disease lies ingrained in his system. The anniversary of the date of the partition is a day of mourning. The shops are closed, and all business is suspended. The people go about the streets barefooted, interchanging amongst themselves the mystic ribbon of eternal love, and the vow to carry on the agitation from generation to generation until the partition has been abolished.

I ask you, ladies and gentlemen, is it right to allow a grievance of this kind to fester in the depths of a national life? The longer you permit it the wider becomes its mischievous operation and the deeper grows the discontent. (Hear, hear.) They say it is a sentimental grievance. Be it so. A sentimental grievance is one which is worthy of consideration. What, I should like to know, would be the feelings of the people of England, under the identical circumstances. But far more so is the question of sentimental feeling important when it is a question of governing an Oriental nation. (Hear, hear.)

But ladies and gentlemen, this grievance is more than a sentimental grievance, and I desire to lay before you some of the most practical considerations which ought to operate for a modification of this partition. The partition was entered into in the name of efficiency. No finance, I venture to hope, is a crucial test for efficient, administration. (Hear, hear.) What, however do you find with regard to Bengal? It is a bankrupt province, unable to meet its demands, and compelled to rely upon subsidies from the Government of India in order to supply its most urgent needs. (Hear, hear.) If Bengal remained united she would have been financially prosperous, and financial prosperity means posperity all round. (Hear, hear.) Let me take another consideration, and not a sentimental consideration. For generations the Hindus and Mahomedans have lived together in peace, but the partition has thrown the apple of discord into their midst, and has created an alienation of feeling which has led to great disturbances and breaches of the peace. Lord Ripon, of blessed memory, strongly condemned the partition on the ground that it had caused deep discontent among the population—meaning the population of which I have the honour to belong. Contentment of the people is the strongest asset of the British Government. Great Queen Victoria taught us the utmost importance of this in the proclamation of 1858, which she closed with these words : "In the contentment of our people lies the strength of our rule." (Hear, hear.) It is useless for me to disgiuse the fact that universal contentment in Bengal has become a thing of the past. Any one who knows Bengal will tell you that it is a province of peaceful people. Why, then, is it now the centre of disaffection and discontent? It is the partition. (Hear, hear.) I have, ladies and gentlemen, the confirmation of official testimony. You will remember that the persons in the Alipore bomb case were charged with conspiring against his Majesty, and it was stated that the day fixed upon was October 16. That date is important because it happens to be the date of the partition of Bengal. (Hear, hear.)

I think, therefore, the partition stands confounded from the mouths of those who support it. What does Lord Morley say? I desire to speak of him with the utmost respect; I have read his works again and again, and I teach them to my scholars and saturate their minds with lofty principles of political wisdom. (Hear, hear.) But if I respect Lord Morley, I love my motherland far more. (Hear, hear and applause.) Therefore, in the interest of my native land, I must enter into the arena and contend against my political guru. Lord Morley says it is merely a matter of the adjustment of boundaries, and yet he also says that the partition is a settled fact. (Hear, hear.) A statesman need not be logical, but he is bound to be reasonable and just, and cannot override the paramount claims of the people. Righteousness is the vital breath of Imperial statesmanship, and a single act of unrighteousness is more disastrous to British rule in India than a great reverse sustained upon an Asiatic battlefield. (Hear, hear.) I cannot conceive anything more disastrous to the credit of the British administration than such a proceeding as the partition. It is calculated to shake Indian confidence in the integrity and sense of fairness of the Government. (Hear, hear.) Lord Morley says the partition is a settled fact. Then I say on behalf of my fellow-countrymen that we decline to accept it as a settled fact. We decline to accept what is admittedly a blunder and what we feel to be a cruel law and a wrong to the sentiment of the people. (Applause.) We will continue this agitation, and we want your sympathy in our great struggle. (Hear, hear.) Will you extend to us the right hand of friendship and sympathy in this matter ? (Cheers.) That this is a deplorable blunder has become obvious by the supplement of a policy of oppression which has become necessary to combat the feeling which has been evoked. Take away this partition and then the oppressive policy will become unnecessary.

So far as this policy of repression is concerned I say this, it came to us in the light of an unpleasant surprise. We are accustomed to associate English administration, especially control by the Imperial Government, with the most scrupulous observance of the rights of personal property. Your history and literature and poetry are saturated with the rights of personal liberty. (Hear, hear.) No one could read the glowing pages of English history without imbibing a passionate love for such liberty ; yet it would seem that we are not to be allowed to enjoy it. By secret reports of a secret police the sanctity of our homes is invaded, domiciliary visits are made, and nine gentlemen, some of them men of light and leading, are wrested away from the bosom of their families and held in detention in gaol under personal discipline, without the purpose being communicated to them, any explanation given or a chance given of making a defence. ("Shame.") And what is the character of these police ? The most unscrupulous in the world. (Hear, hear.) Sir Lawrence Jenkins, the Chief Justice of Bengal, in the Court of Appeal, found that the police had deliberately put a bomb in the house of the accused with a view of fabricating evidence, and Mr. Weston, Magistrate of Midnapur, caused the arrest of the father of one of the accused with a view of extorting a confession. ("Shame!") It is a shame, and it is a matter of bitter irony that these things should be done under a Government presided over by a Secretary of State of the pronounced liberalism of Lord Morley. (Hear,

hear.) "Liberalism," said Mr. Gladstone, "was trust in the people, tempered with discretion." Such proceedings as this, however, involve the gravest distrust of the people, and if you will not trust the people they will not trust you.

"Coercion is an evil instrument of government," said Edmund Burke in the eighteenth century, and so said John Morley in the nineteenth! It exasperates and does not salve, but leaves wounds which take years of conciliatory administration to heal. How did you pacify India after the Mutiny? You did so by the rejection of all coercive measures and by the application of conciliatory methods. (Hear, hear.) With all the emphasis I can command, in the name of common sense, on behalf of the people of India and the credit of British rule, I do earnestly appeal to you to do all that lies in your power to bring about a speedy abrogation of this oppressive partition, which sits like a nightmare upon the troubled bosoms of our people; and might I also be permitted to make another appeal to you, not to accept the official version that the feeling against the partition is on the wane. (Hear, hear.) The patient himself is the best judge of the painfulness of his malady, and we are the patients in this instance. (Hear hear.) My countrymen are suffering, and in their name and upon their behalf I urge you to do all in your power to bring about a modification of the partition of Bengal. I am sure my appeal will not fall upon heedless ears, but will go forth from this meeting accompanied by a volume of sympathy which will have the effect of redressing our grievance and restoring many millions of my countrymen to contentment. (Applause.)

THE POLITICAL POSITION IN INDIA

AT THE NEW REFORM CLUB

Mr. Surendranath Banerjea delivered an address on "The Political Position in India" at the New Reform Club, with Sir Henry Cotton, K.C.S.I., M.P., in the chair.

MR. SURENDRANATH BANERJEA, whose rising was loudly applauded, said: Mr. Chairman, ladies and gentlemen, my first words will be words of acknowledgment and gratitude for the kind terms in which you, sir, have spoken of me. I desire to say this, that I have devoted the best part of my lifetime to the service of my motherland, and so long as I have health and strength to endure they will be dedicated to the service of that motherland. (Cheers.) We are passing at the present moment through a crisis of the greatest magnitude, and it is necessary for all of us to put our heads together for the purpose of devising means for the rescue of our country from the perilous position in which she is placed at present.

You are aware of the policy of repression which has been enforced in Bengal now for over twelve months. With regard to that policy, rendered necessary by the partition of Bengal, I will say no more than this, that it has come upon us, as an educated community. as a most painful surprise, for we have been accustomed to associate English administration, especially when controlled by a Liberal Government, with the most scrupulous observance of the principles of personal liberty. (Hear, hear.) The history and the literature of England are imbued and saturated with the spirit of personal liberty, and we have now to deal with men who have no longer any regard for it. There has been an invasion of that sacred right in the policy of repression—house searches, domiciliary visits by police, repression of public societies by the order of the Executive Government, and last, but not least, deportations without trial. These are the main features of that policy. It is upon the secret reports of the secret police that the sanctity of our homes is liable to be invaded. Domiciliary visits are to be made, associations are to be suppressed on the secret reports of the secret police. And lastly, it was upon the secret reports of the secret police that the nine Bengal gentlemen were arrested, snatched away from the bosom of their families, kept in jail without any charges brought against them or communicated to them, and without being allowed any opportunity of explanation or defence. What, sir, is the character of the secret police upon whose reports these things are done? In the Midnapur appeal case, which was heard by Sir Lawrence Jenkins, the Chief Justice of Bengal, his Lordship said—I am not giving his actual words but their substance—that he accepted the theory of the defence, namely, that the police put a bomb in the house of one of the defendants, and thus fabricated evidence. In the same case Mr. Weston, who was in charge of the prosecution, a high English official, had caused the arrest of the father of one of the accused with a view to obtaining a confession from the son.

It is this police which is to assume the further

charge of repression by the new legislation. You, sir, have given the outlines of that legislation. The police, without any order from a Magistrate, upon their own initiative and responsibility may arrest any person they please, and they will be indemnified by the Act for these arrests. Further, it will be allowed to prohibit public meetings, private meetings, processions, singing on the public streets, illuminations, and what not. I think, sir, I have no need to tell you the genesis of that legislation. August 7 is approaching. It is a memorable day in the annals of Bengal. It is the day of celebration over the whole of Bengal inspired by the partition of Bengal. Thousands, tens of thousands, hundreds of thousands of my countrymen on that day will assemble for the purpose of renewing their vow to continue the agitation against the partition of their country. The Government does not want that. It has committed a huge blunder. Lord Morley has told us it is a blunder and has further told us it went wholly and decisively against the wishes of the majority of the people concerned. Yet it is to be treated as a settled fact. We decline to accept the partition of Bengal as a settled fact (Applause). We will not accept it as a settled fact. So long as it is given to us to agitate, so long as the breath is left in us to cry out, we shall condemn this act as an act of autocratic irresponsibility, thrust upon us because we were powerless to fight the battles of our country. (Applause.) This celebration is going to take place on August 7. From the newspapers that have reached me I find there were grand preparations being made for this celebration. The Government assumes that the demonstrations will take place, and therefore has introduced this legislation. If they wanted to stop the celebrations the easiest and perhaps the wisest thing would have been to modify the partition of Bengal There would have been no celebrations at all. (Applause.) Or, if there were celebrations, they would have partaken of the character of demonstrations of rejoicing and not of mourning, of joy, not of sorrow, of enthusiastic gratitude that would have swept away all the bitter recollections of the past.

Instead of removing the causes of the present discontent, as Sir Charles Dilke suggested the other night, by a few conciliatory measures, the Government is bent upon suppressing outcry and the expression of public opinion. It wants to destroy the danger signals and sit upon the safety valve. (Hear, hear.) What will be the result? Our discontent will be driven inward until it festers in the body politic, and secret societies, the pests of civilised communities which do not enjoy the blessing of free speech and discussion, will spring into existence. What will happen? More oppression, more deportations, more arbitrary measures. What will be the end of this? I desire to put this simple question. Are you going to have in India a greater Ireland, with all the disturbance and excitement and bitterness and organised difficulty that you had across the water? The talk is of the suppression of public meetings. What can be more calculated to emasculate the public life of the country? This is a Liberal Club—I suppose I am right in taking it to be a Liberal Club. I ask the Liberals present here whether they are prepared to countenance the proceedings so utterly in conflict with all the professions of Liberalism? (Cries of "No.") As regards private meetings, the interference of the police, the prospect of such interference by the police fills me with the deepest apprehension and anxiety. In all Hindu households private meetings take place almost every day in connection with marriage ceremonies and what correspond to baptismal ceremonies—it is not baptism, and you would not understand our word describing it, therefore I use the word baptism. In connection with these ceremonies these meetings are held and the thousand and one rites which form the incidents to human life. Are we to understand that the sanctity of our homes and the sacredness of our religious rites are to be interfered with by the myrmidons of the police? No sentiment is deeper in the mind of the Hindu than that associated with home and religion. I desire to raise my warning voice against the dangerous game upon which the Government is embarking. It is playing with fire, and we shall not be responsible for the consequences. (Hear, hear.) It is a most serious matter, this legislation upon which they are embarking. I hope and trust, as the result of the pressure which your Chairman and other Members of Parliament will be able to bring to bear upon the Government, this piece of legislation will be withdrawn and our country may be permitted to go on with the celebrations on August 7. (Hear, hear.)

An outstanding feature of the situation to-day in India is undoubtedly Lord Morley's reform scheme. There are conflicting opinions with regard to that scheme. One class says it is opposed to all traditions, and that it is useless; that it is not worth the paper it is written on; that it has not the elements of a genuine reform scheme; and that such merits as it possessed have disappeared in the arrangement for a system of class representation. On the other hand, others say it attains a level of concession that has never been set before and never even demanded. The truth, as in all such cases, lies in the middle. (Hear, hear.) It is neither one nor the other. We have accepted it—I am speaking of the great Constitutional Party in India—as a beginning, only as a beginning, but a beginning which in the process of evolution will give us a real, definite, effective measure of self-government. The goal of all our aspirations is self-government within and not outside of the Empire, self-government as in the Colonies. It does not spring from the idea of disintegration. We want a closer union. We want the intimate incorporation of India in that great confederacy of free institutions of which England is the august mother. (Applause.) If England wants her rule in India to be permanent, self-government must be accepted. Self-government is the cement of the Empire. It is self-government that has drawn her Colonies around her. Self-government in India will be broadbasing the Empire, basing the Empire upon and tending to unite the mind and the affections of the multitudinous people in the Empire. (Hear, hear.) It has been said to us that as yet we are unfit for self-government. Ladies and gentlemen, the practice of self-government is the best school. (Loud cheers.) It is the best school for the development of that responsibility, and the institution of self-government is calculated to create in us those qualities which constitute the brightest careers in the nation. I deny the contention that India is unfit for self-government. I claim that India has been the cradle of self-government. When the modern world of Europe was sunk in the depths of primeval darkness, with no Government to speak of within this wide continent, before Rome had been built, before Babylon and Nineveh had emerged into the historic arena, our fathers had founded these village communities which long survived the vicissitudes of time. The traces of them are still to be found amongst ruins and decay. (Hear, hear.) They were self-governing institutions, it my be in a limited sphere. Nay, more, I claim that India is the home of that democratic sentiment which is the life of our Parliamentary institutions, and which has done more than anything else I can think of to promote the cause of human liberty and the highest interests of human beings. "Wherever five men are gathered together," says the Indian adage. "the Divine Presence is felt." Where five men are gathered together for a public purpose the Divine Presence is there. According to our ideas, therefore, in all our public discussions on public questions the ever-present Spirit of the Divinity abides. I say that is a noble spiritualisation of the democratic sentiment. It is no longer of the earth earthy. It is transferred to a loftier plane, uplifted to a higher atmosphere, where the things of the material world come face to face and into contact with the invisible things of the spiritual world. (Hear, hear.)

To say to the descendants of these men who could make use of such ideas that they are unfit for self-government, that they have some indelible mark of national degradation, that after a century of British rule they have fallen from their lofty ideals to that point—is to imply the greatest reflection upon British rule. I decline to plead guilty to that charge of national degradation or to admit that a period of British Government has deprived us of the elements of intellectual and moral worth. Try us. (Hear, hear.) Give us an opening, a fair opening. We have been tried and have not been found wanting. You gave us local self-government. For twenty-five years it has been in our midst, and has been a great success. Sir Henry Cotton said so in his admirable minute as Home Secretary of the Government of India in the year 1895, I think. These representative institutions in the elementary stage have been at work in our midst. Extended councils have been in our midst since 1893, and they have also been a success. And wherever amongst Oriental nations Parliamentary institutions have been tried, they have proved to be a benefit to the people and the Government. The Mikado conceded Parliamentary institutions at a time when it was believed that Japan was unfit for Parliamentary institutions, and these institutions have contributed to uplift Japan to the great place she to-day holds among the nations. Turkey has demonstrated her fitness. (Applause.) She has self-government by an Executive, and men in the fever heat of revolutionary excitement have shown all those qualities of restraint, prudence, and moderation which are the crowning attributes of public life and the buttress of Parliamentary institutions in all parts of the world. China is waiting for the consciousness of the immense potentialities of self-government, and last but not least, Persia—(loud applause)—gallant Persia, has raised upon the reins of despotism a constitutionally formed Government, broad-based upon the will of the people. In India they feel that they will also be embarked on that great wave which is sweeping from shore to shore. We should be false to ourselves, false to the culture and traditions of the past and to the modern culture which we have imbibed in such a large measure if we did not feel that revival by the example of the great Oriental nations struggling for constitutional freedom. They have become instinct with new life. New ideas have taken possession of our minds, new impulses, a new spirit is visible amongst us. Is that any reason why we should not turn our eyes to the sun rising on Japan, which will soon pass in its meridian splendour over our heads ? (Hear, hear.) These are our aspirations and hopes, and if at present they may not be fulfilled, though dark clouds may gather, we will cherish these hopes and aspirations with the passionate enthusiasm of our race. They may even fade away like the baseless fabric of a dream and leave not a wreck behind, but none the less we shall cherish that patriotic enthusiasm ; and surely the day will come, under the blessing of Almighty God, when self-government will be established as a fact amongst the people of India. (Applause.)

Let me now say one or two words with reference to the partition of Bengal. No Bengali can speak at any time without referring to the partition. At any rate, I cannot. It fills the whole of my vision, the whole of my mind. The partition of Bengal is our greatest grievance, the root of all our grievances. Lord Morley has told us he will be no party to any modification—I beg his lordship's pardon; I should say reversal; because I hope he will consider proposals for the modification of it. (Applause.) If anybody were to say there was no hope for the modification of the partition of Bengal, I would tell him there was no hope for the conciliation of Bengal. Some people have asked me, because the English people are really not always able to grasp the situation in India, "What is the real grievance?" They have said, "Isn't it merely a division, and one part is governed by one set of officials, and the other part by another, what is the grievance?" We have a substantial sentimental grievance; a very substantial grievance. It is a grievance we can feel. It is not only a sentimental grievance, it is a plan which has been condemned by almost every responsible administrator who has ever gone into the subject. My friend the Chairman has condemned it in the strongest terms, and no one in England is entitled to speak with greater authority on Indian affairs than Sir Henry Cotton. (Applause.) Lord MacDonnell has said it is the greatest blunder committed since the battle of Plassey. That is a sort of Irishism, because Plassey was not a blunder. (Laughter.) The late Lord Ripon has admitted that it caused widespread discontent and disloyalty to British Government. Could there be a stronger condemnation than the fact that the other day men who are authorities in several branches of Indian administration vied with each other in denouncing this child of their own? Lord Curzon, the other day, threw it upon Lord Ampthill; Lord Ampthill cast it upon Lord Midleton; and Lord Midleton threw it back upon the floor of the House. It is going about seeking for its father and finding none. (Loud laughter.) I appeal to you to do everything in your power to bring about the modification of the partition, and re-establish peace and tranquillity in my district of the country; and, further, to do your part to bring about the speedy abolition of these repressive measures which give to an unscrupulous police a very dangerous power. The Chairman has said this is a farewell meeting. So it is. This is the last opportunity I shall have of addressing a public meeting, and I desire to express my sense of gratitude to the British public for the consideration and courtesy with which I have been treated throughout. It has made a deep impression upon me, and I am sure it will be appreciated by my countrymen, and I take it as a proof not only of personal kindness, but of the abiding love and sympathy for that great and ancient race to which I have the honour to belong. One word more. I want to express some words of acknowledgment to the gentleman connected with the newspaper INDIA. (Applause.) INDIA is bravely and vigorously fighting out the battle in England. It is doing splendid work, and I hope and trust it is read, and will be read, by every one of you here, for in its pages the great British public may rely upon finding an organ expressing the best and most thoughtful and genuine Indian opinion upon the matters we have most deeply at heart. (Hear, hear.)